MULTIPLE PSYCHOTHERAPY
The Use of Two Therapists With One Patient

Rudolf Dreikurs, M.D.
Bernard H. Shulman, M.D.
Harold H. Mosak, Ph.D.

ALFRED ADLER INSTITUTE
OF CHICAGO

D0916616

Library of Congress Catalog Card Number 84-71164

Printed in the United States of America
ISBN 0-918560-31-4

Alfred Adler Institute of Chicago, Inc.
159 North Dearborn Street, Chicago, Illinois 60601-3597

Preface

Multiple psychotherapy is a treatment form which uses more than one therapist with an individual patient or patient therapy group. It is not in common use in private clinical practice, but can be found more and more often in clinic and training settings and in some group practices. A number of workers in this field have contributed to the literature on the subject and our book begins with an overview of this literature of the views expressed. We have then provided a description of our own theoretical approach to psychotherapy before we describe the ways we use it and the advantages we have discovered in this method for treatment and training. The latter part of the book consists of segments from actual interviews which display the method. These segments are accompanied by our own comments in order to better show how the process works.

The issues surrounding multiple therapy which we have discussed in this book include its indications and contraindications, how the therapist relate to each other, how the patient relates to each subject and what the small amount of research that exists on the subject seems to indicate.

Rudolf Dreikurs (1897-1972) was our teacher as well as the author of a good portion of this book. In 1946, when he began to use multiple psychotherapy in private practice, such a technique was unusual. At that time the private practice of psychotherapy was usually conducted only in the recesses of private offices. Dreikurs, however, was continuing an approach which he had learned in Vienna before World War II. He had already used group psychotherapy during that period and in addition had worked as part of a therapist duo in the child guidance centers which had been established by Alfred Adler and his co-workers in the Vienna school system. There may have been something about the Viennese experience itself which fostered such an attitude, since other Viennese therapists, such as F. Perls, the Gestalt therapist, and J. L. Moreno, the psychodramatist, showed a similar inclination to move psychotherapy out of the recesses of the private office.

Dreikurs wanted to bring psychotherapy into the open, to make it a community issue. He felt this would help the patient – would bind him more to the community and thus reduce his tendency to feel alienated and separated from his fellows.

An informative parallel can be drawn with the history of confession in the Catholic church. Originally, confession was a public act ("Confess your sins to one another and pray for one another" – James, 5,16). The early Christians confessed to each other at the Sunday liturgy in an atmosphere of caring and were forgiven by the community. Private confession and penance did not become common until several centuries later in response to new social conditions. Confession then became secret.

What we today call psychotherapy began as private meetings between a patient and a therapist. The material discussed was considered too secret to be shared with others.

The burgeoning of various group therapies in recent years indicates that psychotherapy is now seen in a much different light. Multiple psychotherapy, over and above any other advantages, is part of this movement in the direction of conducting psychotherapy in more open settings.

Our experience with multiple psychotherapy as a treatment and training method now encompasses over thirty years for each of us. We would like to share this experience with a wider audience.

In addition we would like to express our thanks to those who patiently prepared this manuscript through our many revisions: Birdie Mosak, Harriet Weichman, Ann Rimland, Fay Grill, and Rose Fenz.

BHS
HHM
1980

Table of Contents

Chapter 1

An Introduction to Multiple Psychotherapy

The Origins of Multiple Psychotherapy

Multiple psychotherapy (sometimes called co-therapy) is a form of psychologic treatment in which a patient or group of patients is treated by more than one therapist. Its earliest reported use was in clinic settings. In the child guidance clinics of the Vienna school system conducted by Alfred Adler and his associates in the 1920's and 1930's, children and parents were counseled in a quasi-public setting which contained a participating audience of school teachers and other parents (Seidler & Zilahi, 1930; Ganz 1953). In these guidance clinics parents and children were counseled jointly by a psychiatrist and a second counselor, either a social worker or a teacher. The client's problems were discussed in his presence by the counselors whenever emotional blocking or resistance prevented a direct approach. It is reported that children, in particular, responded more readily when explanations of their behavior and suggestions for possible changes were not directed at them, but were discussed in their presence.

The first to discuss the use of two therapists in group therapy was Hadden (1947) who claimed that this was a useful way for a more experienced therapist to teach trainees how to do psychotherapy. The two therapists were thus teacher and pupil in their own interpersonal relationship. The first publication which describes the use of the technique in the treatment of one individual patient was by Reeve (1939). In a sensitively written paper, Reeve described his reason for using "joint interviews" in the treatment of individual patients at Mt. Sinai Hospital in Cleveland. His paper discusses many of the fears and objections offered by professionals who were wary of the method and he pointed out what others have found to be true — that the patient is much more willing to accept the method

1

than are professionals who have been trained solely in individual one-to-one methods.

An early use of multiple psychotherapy in private practice seems to have been by Dreikurs (1950) who described the serendipitious origin of his use:

"The first introduction of multiple psychotherapy into the writer's private practice was the result of an emergency. It became necessary to train an assistant to take over the practice for a contemplated absence of the writer. Each patient was seen with the new psychiatrist when the patient's problems, progress and difficulties were discussed in a joint session. Afterward the new psychiatrist made a few individual appointments, the results of which were again discussed in a joint interview. This permitted a smooth transfer of all cases under therapy to the new therapist. This procedure proved to be so effective that it was continued after the emergency period ... "

Dreikurs and his co-workers thus began to use multiple psychotherapy as a regular technique so that the great majority of the patients in this practice were treated by this method. Out of this experience of over three decades, the present volume grows.

Important early writers on the same subject was Carl Whitaker, et al (Whitaker, Warkentin & Johnson, 1949, 1950) who began to use multiple psychotherapy at the same time as Dreikurs, if not earlier. These writers pointed out that the "triangular interview" was useful for resolving a therapeutic impasse, but required the therapists to have a cooperative relationship with each other.

Literature on Multiple Psychotherapy

The literature on multiple psychotherapy is not large. Among more recent papers that review the literature, one such paper (Treppa & Nunnelly, 1974) contains 27 references on the subject while another (Watterson & Collinson, 1976) contains nineteen. In addition, the reports are almost all anecdotal and intuitive with few empirical studies and no statistical evidence that compares multiple techniques to traditional one-to-one methods or shows that it is a method of training psychotherapists which is superior to other methods. The early papers previously mentioned all described personal experiences with the method and claimed usefulness for it, both for training and for psychotherapy. Later papers began to make more specific claims concerning indications for its use, expected results with different categories of patients, the importance of heterosexual pairing in the two therapists, advantages for resolving impasses and the increased potential for continuing personal growth and skill development in the therapist. The most complete review seems to be that of Treppa (1971) with its 41 references.

Training of Personnel

Several anecdotal reports of the use of multiple psychotherapy in training have appeared since 1947. Hadden (1947) used a co-therapist in group psychotherapy for this purpose. Haigh & Kell (1950) stated that multiple psychotherapy could make its greatest contribution in the area of training and research. Hill & Worden (1952) described a method of training psychiatric residents using the technique, while Lott (1952) used it to train clinical psychologists. Yalom and Handlon (1966) described the use of a group of psychiatric residents in training working together with two faculty members and one patient.

Subsequent publications do not usually make explicit reference to its use as a training device. It is as if the method had become accepted as a useful way of training personnel to do psychotherapy and there was no further need to justify its use for this purpose. The two junior authors of this volume were both trained this way by the senior author and have since then used it to train others. In our opinion there is no better way for teachers of psychotherapy to model their techniques for students, although whether it is the best way for teachers to observe their students in action is still open to question, since students may well constrain their behavior and remain overly compliant in the presence of the teacher.

Indications for Use

Whitaker et al (1949) specifically recommended introducing a new therapist as a consultant in order to help resolve a psychotherapeutic impasse. Dreikurs felt it was indicated in the psychotherapy of most patients as a way of facilitating treatment (Dreikurs, 1950; Dreikurs, Shulman & Mosak, 1952; Dreikurs, Mosak & Shulman, 1952). Others who reported that treatment was facilitated include Greenbank (1965), Weisfogel

3

& Sirota (1968), Wainwright (1966), Lehrman (1963), Dyrud & Rioch (1953), Treppa & Nunnelly (1974), Watterson & Collins (1976), and Peven (1977).

Several authors have offered specific indications for its use in certain types of patients. In discussing the use of a public setting in the Vienna child guidance clinics, Seidler & Zilahi (1930) mentioned that the child was often stimulated by the public character of the procedure where he was treated as an equal. Hayward, et al (1952) considered the technique to be particularly useful in treating psychotic patients because it permitted the patient to be more direct in expressing intense feelings and integrate them. Treppa and Nunnelly (1974) claimed that four types of patients particularly suited for multiple therapy, according to their interpersonal dynamics; the distrustful patient, the patient with identity problems, the deprived patient and the emotionally labile patient. Watterson & Collinson (1976) could not replicate the findings of Treppa & Nunnelly and also found in their study that it contributed little to the psychotherapy of the nine schizophrenic patients in their study.

Relationship Between Therapists

Whitaker, et al (1950) encouraged the two therapists to participate actively in the treatment, even to the extent of disagreeing with each other. Similarly, Dreikurs (1950) encouraged open discussion between the therapists in front of the patient to prevent frustration in the therapists and produce a sense of equality in the relationship for all concerned. Haigh & Kell (1950) described how they "struggled to achieve an equalitarian relationship between the therapists." They added that feelings of competition, hostility, dominance and submission to the point of withdrawal "must be faced honestly and openly or probably little therapy is possible for the client and not much learning by the counselors." In the interview, the two therapists are forced to become more aware of their own and the other's strengths and weaknesses as well as learning from each other. Haigh & Kell recommended post-therapy sessions with a playback of a recording of the interview with the client. Warkentin, et al (1951) described difficulties arising from blind spots in the therapists that interfered in the therapy: an inexperienced therapist was tense out of his fear of looking bad in front

4

of a senior therapist or was blind to what was going on and injected himself in inappropriate ways. Sometimes two competitive therapists used the patient as a pawn to fight each other. As therapists learned to respect and work with each other, they would become more comfortable and experience personal growth in the situation. Warkentin and his co-authors warn that multiple therapists should have had therapy themselves before they use multiple psychotherapy.

Some authors express the opinion that the two therapists should ideally be of different sexes. Greenbank (1964) advised this, stating that it avoided heterosexual and homosexual panics, diffused hostility and made more obvious the manifestations of transference and ambivalence. Sonne & Lincoln (1966) and Flescher (1966) used a heterosexual team to help the patient relive the early family relationship with "new parents." Dinkmeyer, et al (1979) suggest especially a male-female team would be especially suitable for marriage counseling.

In a sensitively written paper, Getty & Shannon (1969), two psychiatric nurses, discuss the egalitarian relationship in co-therapy. Mentioning that multiple psychotherapy sometimes includes the assignment of roles to each therapist and sometimes uses a senior and junior therapist, they stress that the egalitarian relationship between co-therapists is another dimension. Egalitarian therapists must respect and trust each other and have equal chance to participate. They arrive at decisions jointly and meet before and after their therapy sessions to discuss the case with each other. They learn to view differences between themselves as legitimate and acceptable. They take equal responsibility and collaborate by often having one therapist actively involved with the patient while the other encourages the patient to examine the interaction.

Paulson, et al (1967), in the only retrospective statistical study on co-therapists examined 42 co-therapy teams. They found that therapists who wanted to work together again tended to have the same theoretical orientation, had few interpersonal difficulties between themselves and were satisfied with each others performances. The existence of a personal friendship between the therapists was not a significant factor and junior-senior teams worked as well together as peer teams.

Objections Raised by Various Authors

The authors of various papers on multiple psychotherapy mention objections raised to the technique by others, not by themselves. Since all the authors used the technique, they were all apologists for it and gave testimony to its usefulness. Objections raised and answers to these objectives are given in Table 1-1.

Table 1-1 Objections to multiple psychotherapy and answers to the objections.

Objections	Answers
Children will not cooperate in front of an audience.	Children are actively stimulated to be more interested and helpful (Seidler & Zilahi, 1930).
Therapists will be unwilling to expose themselves to each other	Many therapists will not have this fear (Reeve, 1939)
Patients will be unwilling to accept two therapists	Where the therapists are convinced of the value of the technique, patient reluctance will be minimal (Dreikurs, 1950)
	Where psychotherapy is structured from the beginning as multiple psychotherapy, there is little patient resistance (Dreikurs, Mosak & Shulman (1952)
It is more expensive and requires more professional manpower	Yet it shortens – duration of treatment which lowers expense and reduces costs (Greenbank, 1964)
Two therapists would confuse the patient; the therapists' interpretation would conflict with each other; transference becomes diluted	This would only happen if the two are not working as a team (Haigh & Kell, 1950)

As one reviews the literature it becomes apparent that the listing of objections occurs mainly in the early papers. Later writings say little if anything about objections. It seems that as the use of the technique increased, and it seemed to offer benefits, the objections became muted.

Professional personnel and patients who are concerned that multiple therapy may interfere with confidentially should recall that group therapy poses the same problem. The vast increase in the use of group therapy and the multiplication of group techniques seems to indicate that confidentially is usually not an overriding issue for patients. If patients refuse to enter into the experience, it is simple enough to excuse them from it and use only one-to-one therapy. Some patients have the same objection to group therapy.

Research

Although Haigh & Kell (1950) mentioned that multiple psychotherapy was a good subject for research, such research has been admittedly sparse. In Reeve's (1939) study, he examined his statistics for a period of six years, and found that out of a total of 157 patients who came to his clinic for diagnosis or treatment or both, only three patients refused to accept this method. Reeve took this as a sign that patients accepted the method with little difficulty.

Weisfogel & Sirota (1968) reported an in depth study of their work with one psychotic patient. They described clinical vignettes from the treatment, including verbatim statements and drew conclusions about the helpfulness of the method.

The two most extensive studies extant are of recent vintage. In one study (Paulson, et al, 1976) examined 42 couples of therapists that had worked together as co-therapists for the purpose of pinpointing some critical areas of interaction between therapists. They constructed a 41 questionnaire of mutually exclusive multiple choice questions which was supposed to identify for each therapist the therapist's preception of (1) his own functioning in the group, (2) his co-therapist's functioning and (3) his perception of the patients' verbal and nonverbal behavior in the group. They hypothesized that where therapist and co-therapist perceptions were in agreement, the pair would want to work together again. They discovered that three factors were most closely related to the therapists' desires to work together again: theoretical orientation, the existence of difficulties in the relation between the therapists and perception of one's own and the partner's participation. Couples who wanted to work together again tended to be of the same theoretical orientation, perceived fewer problems between themselves and were satisfied with the behavior of the partner in the therapy setting. One incidental finding was that although males and females were about equally divided in the group, a higher proportion of female couples wanted to work together again as opposed to male-male and male-female teams. The authors offered no explanation for this phenomenon.

Watterson & Collinson (1976) performed another kind of study. They analyzed their own records retrospectively on 56 patients treated by them with multiple psychotherapy. They functioned as a junior-senior team. They raised the question "In what way (if any) did the junior therapist contribute toward the treatment of the patient; or in what way (if any) did her participation hinder treatment?" They found in the records evidence that the junior therapist definitely facilitated treatment in ten identifiable areas which they defined as (1) understanding dynamics, (2) revealing patient's attitudes toward women (3) revealing transference attitudes, (4) lessening therapeutic tension helpfully, (5) increasing such tension helpfully, (6) facilitating confrontation, (7) lessening transference intensity helpfully, (8) perceiving counter-transference problems of senior partner, (9) lessening secondary gain and (10) giving empathic support. In one area they found that the junior therapist inhibited a male patient who had problems with his wife. The overall experience of these therapists was obviously positive.

Their study also found that in their own experience, co-therapy was most useful in treating the borderline personality, less in other disorders and neurotic depression and least in the treatment of psychoses.

What Can We Learn from the Research?

Such empirical evidence as exists suggests merely that multiple psychotherapy can be helpful in psychotherapy, that it is useful in training and that the therapists must be able to align their own goals so that they work well together. The rest of this book describes the particular experience that a group of us have had with multiple psychotherapy, how we use it and why we value it. At this point our experience is of more than 30 years duration and our commitment to it is such that we would not want to practice any other way.

Because our therapeutic orientation is Adlerian, we will begin with a short description of the process of Adlerian therapy and its goals. Then we will describe our own conclusions, how we use the process and give some verbatim reports which exemplify specific issues in multiple therapy.

8

Chapter 2

The Theory of Therapy in Individual Psychology

Theoretical Considerations

The technique of psychotherapy, as developed by Alfred Adler can be classified as an uncovering and interpretative form of therapy. It has much in common with the usual interview techniques of a common-sense approach; but a characteristic method of exploration, interpretation and guidance distinguishes it from other forms of therapy. Like any specific therapy it has its own theoretical framework. The theory actuates specific modes of psychological investigation and reeducation, and sheds new light on therapeutic procedures which are widely used with a variety of rationalizations.

Any psychological theory implies a characteristic concept of man, his functions, his behavior, and its underlying dynamic mechanisms. Adler perceives man as an indivisible social being whose every action has a purpose. This holistic socio-teleological concept characterizes the theory and explains the therapeutic and educational practice of Individual Psychology.

The holistic view of man, which is reflected in the name Individual Psychology, has a marked impact on therapeutic procedure. Exploration and analysis of single psychological mechanisms cannot explain the total individual. In the case of each mechanism man's creative ability permits him to set his goals and to decide which methods of operation he will use to arrive at his goals. Man's creativity offers him an opportunity to create "cognitive maps" (Adler called them life styles) which give the individual reference points, permit him to choose his life destinations and the routes he will take to arrive at these destinations. Man uses his physical, mental, and emotional behavior to facilitate these goal-oriented movements. He uses his abilities in line with his intentions. His mind and body,

9

his thinking and his feelings are at his disposal when he decides, consciously or unconsciously, to move into action.

It does not matter whether the individual is or is not aware of his decisions. Consciousness covers only a small part of all human functions, be they physical or psychological. Man operates on an economy principle. He is aware of what he needs or wants to know. The degree of awareness may vary; there is nothing going on in him that he does not know of at all, and nothing of which he is fully aware.

Man, as a social being, is primarily motivated by a desire to belong. Only within the group can he fulfill himself; outside of it, he is nothing. All human qualities are expressions of social interaction; they indicate movement toward others. The ability to communicate and to participate is inherited as a potential. But social interest which permits and stimulates full social interaction has to be developed. Man's social adjustment, his full participation, his ability to take all the contingencies of social living in his stride without withdrawal, depend on the amount to which he has developed his social interest.

Its development is restricted by feelings of inferiority. All failures and deficiencies, as far as they are not organically determined, indicate an insufficiently developed or restricted social interest, and an exaggerated inferiority feeling. The "ironclad logic of social living" presupposes a status of social equality, particularly in our present democratic era, as the basis for the feeling of belonging. If the individual feels inadequate or inferior to others, then he doubts his place in the group. Instead of moving toward the group, he defends himself against the consequences of his real or assumed deficiency; he may either over-compensate or withdraw. Mental, emotional, or social maladjustment or disfunction result from partial or total discouragement. Terminating his participation and contribution, the individual switches from the "useful" (socially productive) to the "useless" side of life, becoming preoccupied with matters such as his own prestige at the expense of others, his hedonistic pleasures, the successful avoidance of the challenges of life and sharing up his own self-esteem through an overt and covert hostility to others.

Our whole personality is based on a subjective interpretation of life established during the formative years of our early childhood. Personality is the result of training, which is less stimulated by environmental influences than by the child himself in his efforts at self-determination. The child tries to find a place for himself within the family. He proceeds by trial and error, learning from the reactions he encounters, at least as he interprets them. Very early he takes an active part in establishing relationships with the members of his family. He is not merely influenced by them; he creatively influences them through his anticipations and provocations. In this process of mutual interaction, the child develops a concept of himself. He considers certain methods of operation as suitable and within his reach and trains himself to refine these operations. The influence of reinforcement and modeling provide him with a range of possible actions but which action he chooses is influenced more by his subjective perceptions than by anything else. These basic concepts about himself, his world and how to operate in it are the basis of his life style. These notions, convictions and assumptions usually remain unconscious and form the patient's "private logic" (his consensually unvalidated perceptions) which, when understood, serves to explain behavior which violates common sense.

As long as these biases do not interfere with social functioning we appear to be coping with life reasonably well. A "crisis situation" arises when the individual encounters problems with which he cannot cope adequately within his frame of reference, with his particular life style. This inability to function then leads a perception of threat with its emotional upheaval or social maladjustment because of the lack of coping skills or the discouragement about using them (expectation of failure). The main perceptual change sought in Adlerian psychotherapy is change in private logic so that additional coping skills can be learned and used as responses to the stress generated by the increased challenge in the crisis situations.

The Adlerian therapeutic procedure includes the four phases which characterize every uncovering, interpretive form of psychotherapy. They are (1) the establishment and maintenance of a proper therapeutic relationship; (2) the investigation and elucidation of the dynamics of the patient's behavior; (3) showing these dynamics to the patient through various interpretive techniques so that the patient understands himself (insight) and (4) reorientation and re-education. Since all schools have their own concepts of personality development and psychopathology,

11

the goals of investigation, as well as the techniques, show characteristic differences. Consequently, the Adlerian approach is mostly distinguished from others by its psychological analysis and interpretations.

The Therapeutic Relationship

Any form of cooperation requires an alignment of goals. When the goals and interests of patient and therapist clash, no satisfactory relationship can be established. For this reason the therapeutic effort from the beginning is directed toward winning the patient's cooperation for the common task. The maintenance of this cooperation requires constant vigilance during the course of therapy. What is often interpreted as "resistance" constitutes a discrepancy between the immediate goals of the therapist and those of the patient. The patient may actually disagree with certain explanations or he may not want to admit to himself what is presented to him. He may think that the therapist should "make him well" and refuse to do something himself. He may want to put the therapist into his service or feel neglected, overpowered, or misunderstood. In each case the proper relationship must be reestablished, differences resolved, and agreement reached.

This process of maintaining a cooperative relationship is in itself of therapeutic value as part of an educational process. As the patient can accept the therapist's goals, his own goals are bound to undergo a fundamental change. In many instances the patient does not believe that he can get well and occasionally may even be determined not to get well. His unconscious goal in therapy may then be to demonstrate his "good intentions" while actually trying to defeat the therapist, perhaps because the payoffs for being "sick" are greater than those for getting "well." Another patient may have the intention of getting well, of losing his symptoms, but not of changing his attitudes. He may even want to change but without giving up the premises upon which he operates. In each case the therapist must be able to win at least a temporary agreement as to the immediate procedures to be followed in the therapy.

Since therapy requires close cooperation, the therapeutic relationship is for many patients the first good human relationship in which they can engage in give and take with good grace and withstand friction and clashes of interest without disrupting the relationship. An atmosphere of mutual trust and mutual respect characterizes such a relationship.

It is important that the patient feels accepted from the first moment of contact, but also for the patient to feel that the therapist actually understands how he (the patient) feels. In addition the patient needs an anticipation of success in the therapy, although the therapist can insist that no success is guaranteed. This element of anticipation is essential in a good therapeutic relationship. It is often easier to establish it initially than it is to maintain it throughout therapy. Particularly in moments of relapse or at times when a plateau is reached, the patient's belief is eventual improvement and adjustment may be greatly strained. It is in such moments that special efforts are needed to reestablish the proper therapeutic relationship.

Psychological Investigation

The analysis of the patient's personality and his problems is an integral part of our form of therapy. Our exploration has two objectives – to understand the present areas of his functions, his field of operation; and to know the premises on which he operates, that require a study of the past, of his formative years. The impact of his life style with the current situation is responsible for conflict and impasse; for each individual, different circumstances constitute a crisis situation.

Most Adlerian therapists do not structure the interviews. The investigation takes place as therapy progresses. At times the patient expresses himself freely, provides voluntary bits of information, or merely indicates his subjective feelings. The therapist may ask pointed questions, whether to induce the patient to clarify a point in discussion or to obtain information which the therapist requires for his understanding of the patient. Sometimes the therapist may immediately interpret what he perceives; at other times he may wait for an opportune occasion. Much depends on the temperament and inclination of the therapist as to how much time he gives the patient to express himself, how much he structures the interview, how long he waits before he considers a patient ready for an interpretation. Some Adlerians are very permissive and very cautious in interpretation; others are less so.

The present authors employ relatively structured interviews at the beginning of therapy. The initial interview consists of an exploration of the present situation. We encourage the patient to first express himself freely, telling us how he feels, what bothers him, what symptoms or problems he may volunteer. We explore his motivation for seeking treatment, his expectations, and his therapeutic goals. Even during this exploration of what we call the patient's *"subjective situation"* we inject questions to get the full picture of the patient's feelings and complaints.

Unless the patient is too disturbed emotionally or confused, we proceed during the same initial interview to explore his *"objective situation."* This involves an exploration of the patient's functioning in the five life tasks – at work, in his social relationships and in his family, his relationship to the other sex, in his feelings about himself, and in the spiritual or existential realms.

After having established the subjective and objective situation, we link both sets of information with *"The Question";* that is, we ask the patient what would be different in his life if he were well. The answer to this question indicates the relationship between the actual and objective life situation and the subjective complaint or emotional disturbance. It indicates for what purpose the patient is sick, against whom or what his symptoms are directed, and against which social threat or demand he defends himself by being sick.

If the patient's ailment or disturbance is of longer duration, we explore – if possible during the initial interview – the time and situation of the onset of the symptoms. It was then that the crisis situation has developed. If the condition is chronic and the time of onset too far back, then we leave the exploration of that situation for later consideration when a more systematic investigation of the past is undertaken.

After having established the nature of the present problems and having arrived at a tentative understanding of the dynamics underlying the symptoms and complaints, we proceed to explore the patient's personality. According to Adlerian theory, the main elements of personality structure and dynamics can be found in the patient's life style. Our understanding of the life style permits us to understand why the patient's life situation became a crisis situation for him and suggests what aspects of his private logic need to be changed to help him to cope more effectively with the situation.

Exploring the Life Style

The life style consists of a group of convictions which express how the individual perceives himself, how he views life, and how he conceptualizes the relationship between the two. It is the central, enduring core of personality formed during the early years of life. Behavior is consonant with the life style although not dictated by it. The individual chooses behavior which will assist his attainment of the goals inherent in the life style. While how the individual behaves in any situation may be based upon the long range goals of the life style, the individual's short range goals in meeting the contingencies of the current situation may sometimes be more operative. The concept of life style and technique of soliciting it is central to Adlerian psychology. Adler provided a definite technique for a clear understanding of the life style, the person's basic personality pattern. This method has been described and elaborated by Dreikurs (1944), Mosak (1958, 1972) and Shulman (1962).

The concepts about oneself and about life are maintained throughout life although the person remains relatively unaware of the premises which he has established for himself and upon which he acts. A clarification of a patient's life style requires an investigation of his *family constellation*, the interaction within the group into which he was born and his earliest childhood recollections.

More complete descriptions of methods for eliciting the life style can be found in Baruth & Eckstein (1978) and McKelvie & Friedland (1978).

Interpretation

It is self-evident that a certain amount of interpretation coincides with the investigation and analysis. For this reason it is not possible to separate too distinctly the diagnostic and therapeutic aspects of our psychotherapy. Psychotherapy constitutes essentially a learning process. The patient learns about himself, about his motivations, intentions, and goals. In addition to revealing to the patient his life style, the most characteristic aspect of our therapeutic interpretation is the persistent emphasis upon *goals*. While we may explain to the

15

patient how he feels and why, we emphasize his purposes. We confront him constantly with his movements, with his intentions, whether he is aware of them or not and his private logic. We attempt to offset his tendency to find excuses for whatever he is doing, to blame himself without taking on the responsibility, and to put labels on himself instead of understanding the direction of his thinking, feeling and acting.

All experiences of the patient, within the office in his interaction with the therapist and in his life as revealed by his reports, are utilized to explain his goals and movements to him. As often as possible, reference is made to his basic premises, to his life style. After all, an improvement presupposes a change in the life, at least a partial correction of some of the fundamental basic mistakes. The patient is informed about the purpose of his behavior; it is then left to him to draw his own conclusion.

Reorientation

The most important phase of psychotherapy is reorientation. Its extent, intensity, and duration spells success and failure in therapy. Here the skill of the therapist becomes manifest. Even if he has established friendly and warm relationship, even if he understands the patient and conveys his understanding all this is meaningless unless it leads to reorientation.

The dynamic material obtained in therapy is used to motivate reorientation. Adlerian therapy employs a mirror technique, holding up to the patient his goals and intentions, his decisions which lead to his actions, including those from which he suffers. Such interpretation of goals provides a kind of insight which seems to be singularly effective. Introspection as such, recognition of past influences, discovery of heretofore unknown psychological reactions, do not necessarily provide motivation for change nor indicate how a change could be accomplished. This is different in regard to goals. They are subject to change, at any given moment. When the patient begins to recognize his goals, his own conscience becomes one of the motivating factors.

Insight into goals and intentions does not merely have restrictive or inhibitive consequences. The patient who becomes aware of his own power, of his ability to make decisions, of his freedom to move in one or the other direction, is not merely burdened by an increased awareness of his responsibility, but also free of his feeling of weakness, of his doubt in his own ability. Recognizing his power, he can begin to use it in a different and more constructive way.

Encouragement

Insight is only one therapeutic factor. According to Adlerian theory, the corrective endeavor that makes all the others possible is *encouragement*. This includes the therapist's consistent attitude of acceptance, appreciating his worth as a human being and demonstrating faith in him and the expectancy that the patient will be able to change.

Such a procedure is intended to affect the patient's self-concept and move in the direction of increased self-esteem. In this way, the process contradicts those life situation experiences which discourage the patient and lower his self-confidence. For this reason, we do not make a distinction between analytic and supportive therapy. What is called "supportive" seems to be essential for *any* successful therapy, even for psychoanalysis in its original form. Any reorientation in any form of therapy would be unlikely without these elements which constitute a so-called supportive therapy.

Adlerians try to free the patient from destructive social values such as overconcern with personal prestige or fictitious personal superiority and to replace these faulty values with a sense of social cooperation, respect for fellow-humans, social equality and the pursuit of active constructive social participation (to be *with* others rather than alone and to feel a sense of belonging to a human group). This concern with social values is a characteristic of Adlerian therapy and is an important reason for the ease with which Adlerians accepted and promoted the advent of group therapy methods.

Goals of Therapy

In addition to symptom relief, then, the goals of therapy are to help the patient understand the mistakes in his own private logic which have led him into maladaptive behavior, to teach, reinforce and model for him a range of more adaptive percepts and behaviors and to encourage him to accept and cherish himself and others and correct his own mistaken logic by re-examining it and testing it against his newly forming more adaptive percepts. The patient's verbal reports, dreams and new behaviors are evidence that change has occurred. One piece of evidence considered confirmatory by Adlerians is a change in the patient's earliest childhood recollections. As his outlook on self and life changes, his retrospective memory of the past can also change — evidence that the percepts have indeed changed.

Chapter 3

The Process of
Multiple Psychotherapy

A basic assumption in our use of multiple psychotherapy
is greatly enhanced through its use. Multiple psychotherapy
offers benefit to the patient, the therapist, the psychotherapist
in training and to his supervisor. The method has been used
systematically in our practice since 1946, although Dreikurs
was using it as early as the 20's in the Vienna child guidance
clinics. The patient is seen initially by one therapist, usually
the one to whom the patient has been referred. The conduct
of the initial interview has, in addition to the goal of information collecting, the aim of structuring the procedure in terms
of multiple psychotherapy. The method is explained, the advantages are noted, and the patient's questions and objections are
answered. Unless the patient's condition demands immediate
attention to some emergent situation (e.g. danger of suicide,
need for hospitalization), our practice is to begin a study of
the patient's underlying personality combined with a further
investigation of his symptoms and his life situation.

In order to produce an easy transition into the co-
therapy situation, the next meeting is a highly structured interview with the co-therapist and patient alone. At this point,
the co-therapist is functioning in the same way as any
psychologist might when called upon to give tests to a person
who has been sent to him by another therapist. The co-therapist
asks a specific set of questions designed to elicit the information necessary to establish the life style of the patient. This
procedure usually takes two sessions. The subsequent session
is a "joint" interview between both therapists and the patient.
In this interview, the collected material is discussed, the patient is invited to correct material which is erroneous and to
elaborate wherever he wishes. The two therapists then construct
a summary of the main points of the life style, asking the help

19

of the patient in the formulation of the summary. The object in asking for the patient's help is both to enlist the patient as a full participant in the process and to create a life style summary to which all parties will agree so that it becomes a set of statements about the patient that can be referred to as often as necessary during the later process of explaining the patient's behavior to him.

Sometimes a defensive patient rejects aspects of the therapists' formulation which the therapists are quite sure is accurate. Nevertheless, the patients emendations are accepted for the moment and therapists wait for later material to either confirm or deny their own suppositions.

At this point, one therapist (either one) is selected as the active therapist and the other is consultant. The active therapist now sees the patient for a series of sessions and, at regular intervals, the consultant therapist participates.

This process admits of many variations. The first therapist to see the patient may collect the life style material himself and the patient may not meet the consultant until the joint interview (sometimes called the "double"). Consultant and active therapists may switch roles at times and, when indicated, a series of doubles may be scheduled.

Objections to this procedure are encountered mostly if multiple psychotherapy is not used systematically from the beginning. Complaints are not infrequent, particularly on the part of certain types of patients, but their objections are immediately used for further exploration and interpretation of their psychological significance. This procedure not only usually suffices to overcome the objections and win the patient's continuous cooperation, but the process of workout usually leads to further therapeutic progress.

The advantages of multiple psychotherapy apply to all four phases which characterize dynamic psychotherapy.

Relationship

The relationship between patient and therapists is greatly affected by the efforts of two therapists. The patient's willingness to accept a second therapist depends greatly on the self-confidence of the therapist arranging for such a procedure. While resistance was found among the earliest patients with whom we used this method, serious reluctance to accept the procedure is rarely encountered today. If present, reluctance generally persists only until the first joint interview; after the patient has experienced it in the full advantage of this procedure, he is generally willing to accept both therapists. This willingness continues unless the patient becomes antagonistic toward one of the two therapists or impasse occurs. When hostility is involved, it may be directed as easily toward the active therapist as toward the consultant. The dynamics which lead to the resistance are discussed in a joint interview in which the therapist not directly involved can usually clear up the situation. It has nearly always been possible to reestablish the normal procedure of multiple therapy, although the roles of the active therapist and of the consultant may be shifted.

The participation of two therapists in the treatment strengthens the patient's confidence and increases his willingness to accept interpretations. It leads to an atmosphere of greater objectivity, where the personal bias of any participant can be more easily recognized and dealt with. This more objective and impersonal atmosphere does not hinder, but rather enhances, the progress of the therapy.

The maintenance of a proper and friendly relationship between patient and therapist is also facilitated by the differences of the personalities of the two therapists. Each one has different personality traits, some of which are beneficial, some detrimental, in dealing with a particular patient. In almost every case, these variations of personality tend to supplement each other. If a trait in one therapist disturbs his relationship with the patient, certain supplementary characteristics of the other therapist come into play almost automatically, intensifying the effectiveness of the team (Peven, 1977).

Assessment

The analysis of the dynamics of the patient benefits from the consultation between the two therapists. The chances of inaccurate conclusions are diminished as are the dangers of overlooking certain aspects. While, by and large, a more experienced therapist contributes more, it is not unusual at all for a less experienced one to point out mistakes and omissions as noted by Watterson and Collinson (1976). Divergent opinions are openly expressed before the patient. Such differences of opinion need have no detrimental effect on the patient; on the contrary, he appreciates that a sincere effort is being made and finds it easier to accept final conclusions. Too often during individual therapy a patient is inclined to feel that the interpretations given are unfounded even though they may be correct. The discussion between the therapists clarifies to him such interpretation; it is more convincing to the patient and offers a substantial guarantee of an objective evaluation of them. (Whitaker, et al, 1949).

The discussion between the two therapists helps promote insight. Emotional blocks often invalidate or preclude direct interpretation. Interpretation which the patient finds not acceptable may even lead to argument and increase the resistance. Joint interviews are much more effective in such situations than individual sessions. In the latter the patient may force the therapist into a prolonged period of passivity through his resistance. In the individual session, the therapist may have no chance to bring up his point and sometimes may find it even difficult to interrupt the patient's flow of emotionally-loaded speech; in the joint interview, he is in a completely different situation. The most distressed, anxious and restless patient is willing to listen while the two therapists discuss his problems.

Dreikurs (1950) has pointed out that most parents get greater insight into their own problems by listening to the discussion of similar problems presented by others. Similar observations are made in other fields. Lazarsfeld, et al (1944) have observed that passive participation in conversation, i.e., listening to the discussion of others, seems to play an important part in changing and forming opinions. Moreno (1946) introduced in psychodrama the figure of the "auxiliary ego" who, in a "mirror technique," helps the patient to realize his own position and attitude. In the joint interviews the discussion is often arranged in such a way that one therapist presents the patient's point of view, his private logic, while the other offers an interpretation and evaluation.

Gaining insight and reorientation is a learning process. It requires repetitive, but also highly-varied, presentation of the material to be learned. As each therapist uses a different and varied approach based on his personality, the combined efforts of two therapists increase considerably the effectiveness of the learning process.

Reorientation

The period of reorientation seems to be considerably shortened through multiple psychotherapy. Various factors may contribute to the faster progress which has been observed. Some have already been mentioned. The patient's ability to comprehend and to accept insight is increased through the varied approaches; emotional blocks or disturbances in the personal relationship to the therapist are more easily recognized and more quickly resolved. The double interviews are much more dramatic and impress the patient more than a sequence of individual interviews. The periodic recapitulation of the material obtained and of the progress achieved makes considerable impression on the patient. The monotony of repetition, often unavoidable in a series of individual interviews, is interrupted by a constant change of scene, exchange of ideas, and fresh approaches. During individual therapy, therapist and patient may become deadlocked in a point of investigation or discussion, and the therapist may find it difficult to extricate himself. The double interviews always offer new angles and bring the situation into proper focus.

In a double interview several purposes may be accomplished.

1. In many instances the interview serves as a summary or review session. The immediately previous therapeutic work may be summarized or a longitudinal summary may be attempted. Much of the time in psychotherapy the patient understands many of the strands in his personality but has no picture of its total fabric. In the summary interview the strands are woven together. Many patients, encountering a set back in therapy, feel that they are "now back where I started from." The summary multiple interview may help restore perspective.

2. Planning the next steps in therapy with the patient's participation constitutes another use of the joint interview. Since resistance occurs when the goals of therapist and patient are not congruent, resistance can be prevented or eliminated through discussion. From the therapist's viewpoint, when he is unsure how to proceed next, this interview may help eradicate his confusion or uncertainty. At every stage of treatment patient and therapist know the direction in which they are immediately heading. Patient concern as to whether the therapist knows what he is doing is reduced to a minimum. Confidence in the active therapist remains high since the patient has access to on-the-spot consultation.

3. Joint interviews effect smooth transitions. Patients who might ordinarily resist going to group therapy find the transition easier when they have first experienced multiple psychotherapy. When a patient must be transferred from one therapist to another, the joint interview provides the vehicle for making the move less "bumpy."

4. Thorny problems which recurrently emerge in psychotherapy may be tackled in the joint interview. Problems of resistance, impasse, "positive and negative transference," termination, the discouragement of either the patient or the therapist all lend themselves to discussion within the joint interview framework.

Chapter 4

Some Advantages of Multiple Psychotherapy to The Therapist

Multiple psychotherapy has the obvious advantage of offering the opportunity of constant consultation between the two therapists. The therapists can be more sure of their accuracy in diagnosis, interpretation, and choice of procedure. There is constant opportunity to check one's work with patients. This is invaluable for all therapists no matter what the extent of their experience. The consultant therapist can always bring a new, and perhaps corrective, perspective into the therapeutic situation, regardless of whether he is more or less experienced than the active therapist. Multiple psychotherapy is therapeutic teamwork. Its advantages can be seen in the following example:

> Patient A was the younger of two sons. He was ambitious but discouraged at his inability to live up to his high ideals. He had strong feelings of inadequacy in relation to his brother who was a success by conventional standards. The patient had compensated for his feelings of inadequacy by developing higher moral and intellectual standards which, he felt, made him superior to his brother. He made rapid progress in the early stages of therapy, began work enthusiastically, improved his relationship within the family and was having dreams in which he was successful and aggressive. Progress stopped, although neither patient or active therapist knew why. In the multiple interview, the consultant recognized something the active therapist had missed. The patient had made progress because he had stopped trying to live up to his "ideal image," but he had not relinquished his assumption that he was inferior. Progress began again after this interview.

Individual psychotherapy takes place in an artificial atmosphere which may permit the patient to adjust to the limited relationship with one person, often through an emotional involvement. The introduction of a third person upsets this equilibrium and may result in the patient's revealing more of his natural reactions. This permits both therapists to evaluate the patient's attitudes and progress. Patients sometimes remain on very good behavior through a desire to please the active therapist. The presence of the second therapist is often disturbing enough to the structure of the situation so that the patient is more likely to exhibit more fully his disturbed relationships with people.

Patient B was the baby in her family. Being unsure of her own strength she was exceedingly dependent on other people for approval. She was in her late 20's and rather attractive. She had been dating a man for several years. She felt she did not like him well enough to marry him, but could not bear to hurt his feelings by letting him down. In therapy she had difficulty in verbalizing, since she was never sure of the therapist's reaction to what she might say. She was "making progress" in therapy, trying to behave the way she felt the therapist wanted her to. In one of the multiple interviews, the two therapists disagreed on a minor point, and as is their custom, asked the patient to state her opinion. The patient was completely blocked and confused. It was then pointed out to her that she could not talk for fear of displeasing one or the other of the therapists. She could see that the therapists could disagree without hurting each others feelings, but her single, and typical, response was an apology for not being able to say anything. This incident provided the patient with a dramatic experience and permitted her to recognize more fully her faulty attitude.

When a therapeutic impasse arises because of the patient's strong resistance or because the therapist has inadvertently gone up a blind alley or fallen into a non-productive rut, the joint interviews offer a fresh approach, a disruption of a relationship which has become too rigidly set, a reconsideration of issues, and, if necessary, a switch in therapists.

Patient C suffered from feelings of personal inadequacy in any situation in which he could not maintain a position of superiority. After first making progress and improving his personal relationships, he became depressed. At a joint interview, both the patient and the consultant therapist recognized the sibling rivalry that the patient felt to the active therapist, who was the same age as the patient. The consultant therapist was able to clear the air, and, by taking over the role of active therapist, continued to work with the patient until his antagonism was dissipated and he no longer felt that he had to be "more intelligent" than the active therapist, whom he identified with a younger sibling.

Many patients are adept enough to put the therapist into their own service, a performance which is often interpreted as counter-transference. They thus trick the therapist into confirming their own opinions of themselves, while the therapist is trying to help the patient change these self-concepts. When a therapist has "fallen for the patient's trick," the joint interview is often effective in bringing about recognition and correction of this situation.

Patient D, an only child of overprotective and demanding parents, was constantly making a mess of his jobs, his friendships, and his marriage. His interviews usually consisted of a dissertation on the disappointments and failures that he knew he had brought about himself. The active therapist would patiently point out the meaning of his behavior, and how it followed logically from his concept of himself as a person who had no chance in life and who could find glory in catastrophe. In a joint interview, the consultant therapist saw that the patient had succeeded in provoking the active therapist into telling the patient what he was doing that was wrong. The patient had utilized the therapist's responses as further evidence that he was "a guy who couldn't do anything right" and who was "doomed to failure."

Even didactic analysis – of whatever kind – does not completely remove a therapist's bias and emotional blocking; and his strong desire for a patient to get well, or his need to impress a patient (other forms of counter-transference) often interfere with what is therapeutically better indicated. Whenever the therapist becomes emotionally involved with the patient for his own satisfaction, the consultant therapist helps to solve this difficulty through the joint interview, or through taking over the role of active therapist.

Patient E was a depressed young woman who was extremely ambitious and felt "stupid" in spite of her above average accomplishments in her own profession. She could stand no criticism from her husband, responding to his slightest remark with feelings of inferiority and consequent angry outbursts. Her competitiveness extended itself to the active therapist, who reacted by feeling irritated by the patient and being disinclined to work with her. The consultant therapist could show the active therapist the nature of his reactions, and the therapists switched roles. The former active therapist, now in the role of consultant, no longer responded to the rejection by the patient, and the therapy could proceed.

One important element in disrupting the emotional involvement of the therapist is that in joint interview the casual and objective discussion of the patient's problems almost always clears the air and provides a more impersonal atmosphere for any active therapist who has become overprotective, oversympathetic or hostile.

One of the chief values of multiple psychotherapy is found in the numerous opportunities it offers the therapists to play different roles in relation to the patient. Through watching how another therapist meets a situation, the therapist's own vista is broadened, and he can grow through the experience of another therapist. It is a reciprocal process, in which even a more experienced therapist can benefit from the fresh view of a younger man.

In the multiple interviews the therapists can provide a variety of experiences for the patient. One therapist can be more directive, another less; one may be forceful, the other permissive. A special type of situation is one in which one therapist actively interprets to the patient the meaning of his actions, while the second therapist "argues" from the point of view of the patient's "private logic" (playing devil's advocate) as if trying to disprove what the first therapist has stated, or as if making the excuse that the patient himself has made. In such a situation, the patient often recognizes his own faulty perception as he sees the therapist using his own mechanisms.

Patient F was an overprotected child who had felt rejected by her parents and especially by her father. With a permissive and supportive therapist she made very slow progress in gaining insight into the nature of her depressions. The consultant therapist, on the other hand, would make pointed interpretations of the patient's own dynamics, to which the patient reacted with strong resentment and depression. She would have discontinued therapy but for her relationship to the permissive active therapist. The latter refrained from making the interpretations which might be upsetting to the patient. Within this structure, the patient utilized the relationship with the active therapist to work out her reactions to the consultant therapist and to assimilate eventually his evaluation of the dynamics involved.

A patient who refuses to accept an interpretation is more likely to consider it if he finds that a team of therapists in open discussion agree on this same point. His reliance on authority is thus more related to *people* than to a single *person*.

Patient G, a successful business man, was having marital difficulties. He did not see that his rigid critical attitude and assumption of righteousness were significant disturbing factors in the marital relationship. He did not at first believe that what he called "facts" were his own biased perceptions. When, in a multiple interview, both therapists concurred on this point, the patient was impressed enough by the similar and mutually supplementing opinions to consider that perhaps the "facts" were not as he saw them.

Multiple psychotherapy facilitates termination. The constant inclusion of the second therapist prevents two dependent a relationship on one therapist and makes it easier for the patient to carry over his newly found relationship to people other than the therapists. The consultant therapist may, moreover, see aspects of progress or lack of progress that the active therapist has overlooked because of his more intense relationship.

Patient H had been a pampered child who was hampered by his own self-indulgence. He made considerable progress in therapy, changing and improving his attitude and actions. However, he continued to suffer from mild depressions which prevented him from functioning at his to-be-expected level. The consultant therapist saw that the patient was actually prepared to meet his problems on his own, but preferred to use the excuse of being in therapy to avoid unpleasant tasks and situations. A time was then agreed upon with the patient which was to mark the end of his self-indulgence, and the rest of the interviews were spent in summarizing the dynamics and progress of the therapy. After discharge the patient was able to rely on himself adequately.

Chapter 5

Some Advantages of Multiple Psychotherapy for the Patient

As we have already noted, patients accept multiple therapy easily. At first, some are reluctant and others somewhat suspicious. The best way to overcome this resistance is to start multiple therapy immediately by establishing the roles of the two therapists at the beginning of treatment. Once the patient has experienced the technique, he sees its value and accepts the approach. In fact, many patients express satisfaction that more than one person is concerned with their welfare. They feel that they are receiving more service and more variety. Multiple therapy, moreover, prevents the patient from feeling misunderstood or abused by one therapist, in that he can always discuss such apprehensions and feelings in the "multiple session." He is, consequently, less fearful of antagonizing the therapist and can "open up" with a greater feeling of security.

Patients often enter treatment with the feeling, whether it be expressed or not, that the therapist is or should be both omnipotent and omniscient. They hope that the therapist will wave a magic wand and cure them completely and near-instantly. Many do not necessarily want to learn anything about themselves; they just want alleviation of their symptoms. They often ascribe ideal qualities to the therapist and rebel against the idea that the therapist is ungodlike – a human being who makes mistakes, who also has problems. Such concepts are counteracted when two therapists disagree, for the disagreement destroys the projection of omniscience onto the therapist. It makes, of the therapists, not superior beings, but human beings with perhaps a superior knowledge of psychological dynamics, who are interested in helping the patient to arrive at a new understanding of himself with a subsequent reorientation in his behavior.

True learning is an experience rather than a mere accumulation of "facts." This experience is provided by multiple therapy in various ways. It permits the introduction of two personalities with two different approaches to whom the patient can react and with whom he can interact. In this fashion, he learns to modify his expectation about people. His fallacious perceptions of social interaction can be pointed out and evaluated on the spot. He can work out his own interpersonal conflicts in his interaction with the therapists. For example, the patient may make a senior therapist a father figure and simultaneously set up a sibling rivalry situation with the junior therapist. The expansion of therapeutic roles can thus aid materially in the resolution of certain prominent conflicts which trace their origin to the formative years of family life.

> Patient A was the older of two brothers. His father was physically weak, a poor provider, who played a subordinate role in the family. While the younger brother resembled the father, the patient was able to overrun him, being the confidant and helper of mother, and assuming a protective attitude toward his brother. He was in competition with all men he encountered, trying to elevate himself above them. In therapy, he rebelled against the senior therapist whom he put in the role of his father, and was constantly surprised to find himself unable to push him down. The junior therapist was cast in the role of the brother, with the patient attempting to remain one step ahead and resenting the therapist when the latter could hold his own.

The introduction of fresh viewpoints keeps the therapy from getting into a rut and allows the patient to select, to compare, and to assess the material that is discussed in his presence. In fact, even such a simple procedure as one therapist's rephrasing of the other therapist's remarks can make the material more understandable, and consequently, more acceptable to the patient. The patient may gain new insights from the "correction" of one therapist by the other. Certainly, the probability of interpretations being accepted is greater when one therapist independently validates the opinion of the other.

Further, multiple therapy permits the patient to be both spectator and participant. He can be the subject of the discussion and at the same time a more objective viewer of the proceedings. One patient described it as "like watching a ping pong game, only you're the ping pong ball." The patient can observe one of the therapists, for example, play his (the patient's) role and evaluate himself without becoming so emotionally involved that he cannot assess his behavior accurately.

Patient B, a college senior, an only child, who became discouraged in his efforts "to be a genius," had become thoroughly pessimistic during his senior year in college, when he was confronted with the intense competition and the uncertainty of his future. However, he was unable to recognize the defeatist and pessimistic attitude he had assumed. During a joint interview, the active therapist assumed the patient's role and "argued" with the consultant, using all of the patient's rationalizations which seemed to justify his defeatism, while the consulting therapist offered interpretation of the actual motives involved. The patient became able to recognize his motives and his reluctance to participate in life, and became aware of his own resistance against facing his actual and unfounded attitudes. This was a turning point in his development of better social orientation and of an increased ability to function in school.

In individual therapy, should patient and therapist not 'hit it off," the patient may become discouraged sufficiently to terminate therapy. This occurs less frequently in multiple therapy, since the introduction of a second therapist permits resistance to be analyzed more easily in the joint sessions. In the event that resistance becomes so great, all such efforts notwithstanding, that the patient's hostility or distrust prevents positive movement in therapy, the patient can be transferred to the other therapist without feeling rejected or discouraged, or feeling that he has to start all over again.

Dependency, as a factor in therapy, provides many crucial problems for the therapist. These dependency problems require solution throughout the several phases of treatment. In the initial phases, the problem for the therapist revolves about the necessity of helping the patient recognize his own responsibilities in therapy. The patient, on the other hand, partly due to his own personality and partly because of a cultural pattern that the "doctor knows best," seek to rely on the therapist and to be cured by him. During the middle stages of therapy, the patient may vacillate between dependence and rebellion against it; and even the shrewdest therapist occasionally becomes ensnared in the traps of the patient. In the final phases of therapy, the problem of termination becomes prominent. Here the patient must become convinced that he is "graduating" and not being "expelled," that he is ready to meet the world on his own. He must come to realize that, while he and the therapist have been participants in a good relationship, he can now stand by himself.

Multiple therapy facilitates the resolution of these dependency problems. The "doctor knows best" attitude may be discouraged very early, when detected, by a discussion of this attitude by both therapists. It may be pointed out that while the therapist possesses certain professional skills, the patient will play a major role in the therapy; and he comes to assume some responsibility for his own therapeutic growth through his participation in the discussion.

When dependence upon the therapist is intensified in the middle stages of therapy, joint discussions may serve to dissolve this impasse to further therapy. In fact, since the patient deals at the start with two therapists, dependence upon a single person is immediately eliminated. It may be indicated to the patient that he need not rely on any single person, that he can consider "going it alone." The patient may thus be guided from an attitude of dependence to one of interdependence. We have found special merit for this method in dealing with those intense emotional reactions to the therapist which are often called tranference neuroses. Here, by shifting to the "neutral" therapist, these attitudes may be uncovered and faced by the patient with a minimum of fear or guilt. They may be carefully analyzed and interpreted and the transference dissolved.

> Patient C reached a point in therapy where she seemed unable to communicate with the therapist. She felt she was in love with him but felt guilty for having such feelings. After confessing this love to the therapist, she reacted with shame which, in turn, provided another barrier to communication. She had a number of interviews with the consulting therapist, during which she realized that her attitude toward the active therapist was merely a repetition of attitudes toward her father. After this problem was worked out, she was again able to communicate with the active therapist.

Should the active therapist become ill or take a vacation, the patient's dependency needs are less apt to lead to feelings of "desertion." The absence of the therapist merely means that the patient will be consulting with the other therapist for a longer time than usual.

Since all of these emotional attachments can be analyzed and clarified and viewed with proper perspective, termination can be more easily accepted by the patient. Undoubtedly, there may be some regrets about giving up therapy and some experiencing of doubt about functioning on one's own. Nevertheless, the "break" is smoother, for the attachment is to the *situation* rather than to an *individual.*

Finally, the interaction of the therapists provides a social situation of paramount importance. It shows the patient a good human relationship where two individuals can and do have an interpersonal relationship based upon mutual respect. He can observe the cooperation of two individuals, which transcends competitiveness, "power politics," and prestige-seeking. He can see how this cooperation can exist even when the therapists disagree; and, above all, he may learn that one can be wrong without loss of status. This lesson may indeed be of more far-reaching significance for the patient's reorientation than any interpretations referring to his mistaken assumption that to err implies inadequacy or failure.

This procedure has implications beyond individual improvement. It negates the cultural pattern to which the patient succumbs when he assumes that deficiency is degrading and in this way the therapeutic procedure exemplifies democracy in action.

Chapter 6

Relationships Between Therapists and with Patients

Although we have previously discussed some aspects of relationships between therapists and the patient's relationship to the therapist dyad, it seems appropriate to discuss this important issue in more detail.

In one-to-one therapy the number of relationships subject to examination is two. When we add a co-therapist, the number of possible relationships is multiplied. While the number of mathematical combinations remains small, the number of psychological relationships expands in almost geometrical progression. Of this number we shall explore (a) the relationship of the patient to each therapist; (b) the relationship of each therapist to the patient; (c) the relationship of the patient to the therapists as a dyad; (d) the relationship of the patient to one therapist vis-a-vis the other; (e) the relationship of each therapist to the other; and (f) the relationship of each therapist to the other vis-a-vis the patient.

The Relationship of Each Patient to The Therapist

One value of multiple psychotherapy is that it provides the patient with at least two therapeutic relationships. Some of the advantages that accrue to the patient have been discussed in Chapter 5. That part of the literature which comes from the psychoanalytic area discusses patient-therapist relationships in terms of "transference." In its original meaning, transference referred to the analyst being invested by the patient with qualities that belonged to the patient's parents. The patient's childhood feelings about the parent are displaced onto the analyst, both the positive and negative feelings. The "transference neurosis" occurs where the patient becomes more concerned about getting emotional satisfaction from the analyst than about getting well. Resolution of the transference occurs where the analyst successfully traces these feelings back to the infantile conflict while encouraging the patient to recognize, observe and examine his own feelings as displacements. In this way, the analyst sees himself as allying with the healthy and mature aspects of the patient's ego, to help the patient recognize the imappropriateness of such feelings as well as the childhood hurts from which they come.

In time, the term *transference* came to be used as a general noun for two classes of relationships: all those relationships in which the patient's accurate view of the therapist was impeded by the vagaries of the biased perceptions in the patient's own life style and, in general, all relationships in which the patient had strong positive or negative feelings for the therapist.

Thus, Slavson (1960) objected to co-therapists because the transference was "split." Mintz (1963, 1965) argued that this was a benefit of multiple therapy, because co-therapists replicated the two-parent family. Most authors disagree with Slavson (Weisfogel & Sirota, 1968; Hayward, et al., 1952; Treppa, 1971). All of the empirical evidence available suggests that Slavson is wrong.

Where the nonpsychoanalytic literature is examined, it is obvious that all the authors talk about the same observed behavior: ambivalent feelings in the patient, strong liking or dislike for the therapist and misperception of the therapist by the patient. These authors, however, prefer to speak of relationship in general rather than transference. Sonne & Lincoln (1966), using a family therapy approach, prefer the concept that the therapist becomes a significant figure to the patient in his own right, rather than becoming an object for displaced feelings only. Naturally, when the whole family is present at the session, it becomes inappropriate to speak of transference to explain the patient's reaction to the therapist.

While for psychoanalysis the formation of the transference, in its strict sense, is a necessary part of the treatment, for the Adlerian it is an impediment to treatment. The Adlerian wants a good working alliance with the patient with mutual respect, cooperation and complementary goals (the patient wants help and the therapist wants to help him). Adlerians recognize that the dictates of the patient's life style may direct him to repeat with the therapist certain ways of relating that he used with his parents, and that the patient may also develop strong emotional attitudes toward the therapist; but they do not desire such a situation and try to avoid it from the onset. Like Dyrud & Rioch (1953), the present authors believe the multiple therapy is most useful both for preventing the patient from misperceiving or having inappropriate expectations from the therapist and for resolving any impasse that may occur because such an unfortunate event has happened.

Watterson & Collinson (1976) point out that "transference" attitudes in the patient are more quickly recognized and more easily interpreted in multiple therapy. Two therapists may discuss the patient's convictions, their meaning and purpose, in the patient's presence. The therapist who is not directly involved with these feelings may discuss them with the patient while the other therapist observes. The latter may make some observations which eluded him while he or she was working with the patient because while this therapist was working with the patient, he or she was too directly involved to see what was transpiring. Or the consultant therapist may explain to both the patient and the other therapist what he or she thinks has been occurring. Finally, if an impasse cannot be dissolved while the directly-involved therapist is present, the patient can meet temporarily with the other therapist, discuss the impasse, after which therapy can resume with the participation of both therapists.

Hulse, et al., (1956), Sonne & Lincoln (1966) & Mintz (1965) among others comment on the advisability or necessity for providing one therapist of each sex for each patient. Since many practices, private and institutional, could not possibly provide such an arrangement, they either could not utilize multiple therapy or they would have to make other arrangements such as providing multiple therapy for a smaller number of patients than their case load or using same-sexed therapists. While Lundin & Aronov (1952) feel that "Of all the factors operating in the co-therapy method the most outstanding is observed to be the simulated family setting which is created by the presence of two authority figures," they conclude that "our experiences to date indicate that the two therapists need not be of opposite sexes (p. 77)." Their findings, however, are limited to the schizophrenics in their study and may not be generalizable. Most of the comment on opposite-sexed therapists is based upon theoretical considerations rather than upon empirical findings.

In some instances the utilization of opposite-sexed therapists is based upon the expansion of transference relationships. In transference terms the therapists become father and mother surrogates. Another view suggests that if the therapists are same-sexed and the patient is of the other sex, the therapists will not be able to appreciate the experience of the patient since they will not have had the same experiences which their patient has had. Similar arguments have been forwarded by those who advocate that only a woman therapist should or can treat women and that only black therapists can or should treat black patients since a white therapist cannot comprehend the black experience.

We have here a *reductio ad absurdum* argument, for carried to the extreme, only a therapist who had been schizophrenic himself could treat a schizophrenic, and the psychological sequelae of brain damage could only be treated by a brain-damaged therapist. Further, no therapist could treat anyone older than himself, and unmarried therapists would be disqualified from doing marriage counseling, and in most instances from providing childrearing advice to parents. Such arguments deal with probabilities only and ignore the individual qualities of each therapist and patient. Sometimes there are certain situations in which the sex of the therapist may facilitate therapeutic progress or hamper it or even make it impossible. This can often be determined at the beginning of therapy from the patient's early recollections (Mosak, 1965). In these cases, special effort should be made to use the appropriate therapist for the patient.

What then are the different forms of relationship the patient may have to the therapists? He may like, trust, cooperate with and rely on (or the opposite) one, both or none. He may strongly prefer one to the other. He may attack or denigrate one and overrate the other. In essence, he is reacting to two different personalities and so will respond to the traits of each and the therapeutic style of each. Examples of patient responses to one member of a therapeutic dyad are given in Chapters 4 and 5.

The Relationship of Each Therapist to the Patient

Much of what has been said in the previous section can be equally applied to what psychoanalytic theory calls "countertransference." Just as the patient brings his life style to the therapeutic situation, so does each therapist. These life style convictions may result in nonreality-based attitudes toward the patient, attitudes emanating from the therapist rather than appropriately contributable to the patient. The therapist in such a position may be working out his own problems rather than those of the patient. Aside from this, therapist attitudes toward the patient may also be reality-based. The patient may indeed be provocative, annoying, a mischief maker, a demander, a manipulator or one who acts out. The therapist may then become irritated, seduced or manipulated. Theoretical considerations may present another dimension to the relationship. When a therapist assumes that a patient has a poor prognosis no relationship may evolve or be encouraged, and therapy may have a short life since the therapist may have to vindicate his prognostication. A knowledge of one's own life style and inner feelings is propaedeutic to the practice of psychotherapy.

Several authors have agreed that multiple therapy is most helpful in countertransference situations. Whitaker, et al., (1950), Sonne & Lincoln (1966), Dryud & Rioch (1953) and ourselves (1952) all claim that impasse resulting from countertransference is more easily resolved in multiple therapy. Perhaps the claim of Treppa & Nunnelly (1974) is most telling. They point out that the presence of another therapist in the room may by itself greatly reduce the chance that either therapist will get very far in allowing his own personality to impede therapy before the other therapist will intervene. Thus, the three main kinds of countertransference behavior (inappropriate attitudes toward the patient arising from the therapist's own private goals, inappropriate action arising from the success of the patient in manipulating the therapist and the therapist's attempts to fit the patient into his own pet theory) are all more easily resolved in multiple therapy.

Examples of such attitudes and behavior can be found in chapter 4.

The Relationship of the Patient to the Therapists as a Dyad

The relationship of the patient to two or more therapists may reflect both situational and life style considerations. Some patients find that meeting with two therapists poses a difficult problem. They make statements such as "I have difficulty talking with one person. Two is even harder." Often this refers to the situation which differs from that expected or which a patient has already experienced in a previous therapy. Sometimes such statements reflect the cry of the "controller" (Mosak, 1973) who finds it difficult to manage the situation when he encounters two therapists. When the difficulty is situational, one can deal with it through careful structuring, explanation of the benefits, reassurance, making the patient comfortable, going slow until the patient feels more at ease, simultaneously attending to the patient's feelings. When the difficulty is based upon life style, the therapists will deal with the patient's demand to control the therapy situation, for whatever reason he demands such control.

Some patients will experience multiple therapy as benevolent while others will perceive or create it as an adversary relationship. Those who take a positive stand may make such statements as "It's nice to have two people interested in your case." "Two heads are better than one." "It's the first time so many people have been interested in me." "I know that you really want to help me because you lose money when you use two therapists." Those who assume the negative stand may voice it with such statements as "It's two against one." "I don't see why we have to have these double sessions, I do fine with just one therapist."

One of the techniques used in multiple therapy is for the therapists to talk with each other while the patient listens. Many patients welcome this opportunity to momentarily become detached from active participation so that they can listen more freely, free of the necessity to immediately respond. Others become resentful, protesting their being left out. "You make me feel like an object, like I'm not here," they complain. "If I'm a person (a patient), why don't you talk to me directly?" Sometimes an explanation of the procedure will suffice. At other times the therapists may tie this complaint in with the patient's life style. At still other times the therapists may employ this as strategy, as for example, when they wish to help the patient recognize or mobilize his anger (Mosak & Shulman, 1974, p. 54). With some patients they may apologize for the noninclusion and expand the discussion to a three-way conversation.

The discussion above is illustrative rather than inclusive. What is being suggested is that the therapists must always be alert and attentive to the patient's perception of the therapist dyad and will, on the basis of situation and life style, adopt varying strategies to meet the patient's therapy behavior.

The Relationship of the Patient to one Therapist vis-a-vis the Other

As therapy proceeds, patients assume varying stances toward each therapist. Many of these postures are based upon realistic considerations. To illustrate, when the patient sees each therapist individually rather than in a double interview, each may charge a different fee. When this occurs, the patient may wish to work with one therapist instead of the other because the first therapist's fee may better suit his pocketbook. On the other hand, the patient may choose to wish to see the therapist who charges the greater fee because for this patient the fee size is equated with greater competence or experience. This problem is naturally eliminated if both therapists charge identical fees for their individual sessions.

The preference for which therapist to work with individually is often related to the therapist's age and maturity. Some older patients are reluctant to talk with a therapist who is younger than they are. Some patients make their choices on the basis of the type of degree, preferring a psychologist to a psychiatrist or vice versa, based upon whatever expectations the patient has of each profession. The preference may result from expectation ("He speaks with a German accent, and that's the way I always thought a therapist should be"), therapist "strength" ("He never lets me get away with anything, and that's good for me"), feeling understood, the therapist's agreement with the patient, and similar factors. Preferences are probably unavoidable, but the therapists must be careful to avoid traps which the patient may set for them (Mosak & Shulman, 1974, p. 52). While it may be flattering for one therapist to hear that the patient prefers him or her to the other therapist, acceptance of such flattery may have disastrous consequences for the therapy. The dangers of such susceptiblity to flatter have been vividly illustrated by Mosak & Gushurst (1971). Manipulation, seduction and making an individual therapist one's "property" constitute some other traps which patients may create for the unwary therapist and may retard the therapy. Therapists must exercise vigilance, and should these behaviors occur, adopt appropriate measures. Some measures used are the discussion of the maneuvers, the transferring of the patient to the non- or less-favored therapist for the next period of therapy, and more frequent scheduling of double interviews. Some patients may even attempt these maneuvers during the double interview through freezing out the nonpreferred therapist and only addressing their communications to the preferred therapist. They may even turn their backs on the former.

If the patient is adamant about not seeing his second therapist, a crucial problem arises. Discussion may assist the patient to greater flexibility. Such discussion may even uncover a previously unnoticed or unstated problem in the situation or relationship between the patient and the nonpreferred therapist, the eradication of which may place the multiple therapy back on the track. The discussion may be held either in individual or double session. Some multiple therapists maintain such a commitment to multiple therapy as their form of operation that if a patient is intransigent, they will refer the patient to another therapist who engages only in individual therapy. They rationalize this behavior not only upon their therapeutic preference but upon their feeling that to switch the patient to individual sessions would inform the patient that he could not run the therapy. When the patient has "good reasons" for nonacceptance of the second therapist, a third therapist may be substituted, provided one is available. The latter can more often be done within an institutional framework than in a private practice.

The Relationship of Each Therapist to the Other

Since the aim of multiple therapy is to produce a coordinated therapeutic effort, we should examine those factors which lead to this coordination and those that impede or defeat it. Too often therapists delude themselves that they are conducting multiple therapy merely because of the physical presence of two therapists in the consulting room. Yet, occasionally, we may observe that one of the therapists carries the ball while the other therapist sits by passively or takes notes. This situation is particularly prevalent in situations in which one therapist is being supervised by the other and the supervisee retreats into an anonymity in which he hopes not to be evaluated. Another situation we encounter is one in which two therapists are doing individual therapy in each other's presence, sometimes oblivious of each other, sometimes competing with each other. The former may occur under varying circumstances. Sometimes the therapists are not actually committed to the practice of multiple psychotherapy; in other situations the therapists have made the commitment but have not trained themselves to function as a team. Occasionally therapists may pursue a promising lead or interpretation so enthusiastically that they may forget for the moment that they are practicing multiple psychotherapy, one therapist ignoring the other and conducting therapy in the presence of the other therapist. The latter, involving therapist competition, may be observed when therapists actively compete to demonstrate superior knowledge or competence in order to woo the patient's favoritism. The competition may go underground with one therapist, feeling inferior to or intimidated by the other, sitting by silently. While such behaviors may be manifested, they are an uncommon occurrence. Dyrud & Rioch (1953), in their study of multiple therapy at Chestnut Lodge, comment:

> One of the most gratifying positive effects of the multiple therapy experiment was the improved working relationship among staff members. It is our impression that this occurred in every case in our series. The competitive feelings of psychiatrists with regard to their professional skills are likely to be suppressed since competence in this field is associated with maturity which supposedly rises above competitiveness. Thus it is not surprising that the competition in such a collaborative undertaking would take on covert forms, such as working at cross-purposes with the other therapists, attempting to dominate the interview, or withdrawing from active participation. Direct discussion of such maneuvers usually led to a closer collaboration. It is fair to say that the staff as a whole was prejudiced against multiple therapy at the outset. This prejudice had at least two roots. First, the competitive feelings were expressed as apprehension that the other doctors would find out all one's secret faults as a therapist and gloat over one's mistakes. Second, and perhaps more important, was an understandable fear that harm might come from invading the privacy of the one-to-one relationship of individual therapy. When none of these dire consequences occurred, but instead a collaborative effort toward a better integration, the burden of isolation was lifted from the doctors and a greater mutual understanding evolved. (p. 26)

If therapists wish to make a coordinated effort, certain conditions should prevail. First, there is the establishment of a noncompetitive atmosphere between the therapists. The goal of therapy is to help the patient, not to determine which therapist is better or more likable. Therefore, it is important to eliminate feelings of superiority and inferiority from the relationship. While therapists certainly vary in experience, knowledge, and competence, such variations need not lead to these feelings. If therapists recognize that there is no necessary correlation between superiority (or inferiority) and superiority (or inferiority) feelings, they can recognize that their inferiority need not prevent them or discourage them from making a contribution to the therapeutic discussion. They can similarly recognize that their actual superior status need not lead them to show off, to denigrate the other therapist or to disregard his views. A therapist inferior in experience may even move the therapy along more rapidly because in his or her naivete or lack of experience, he or she may ask questions of the patient or of the other therapist which may provide needed clarification for both the junior therapist and the patient. If competitive considerations are eliminated, mutual respect can follow. The reverse is also true for if mutual respect exists, competitive considerations are discarded. This permits communication between therapists to flow easily, and the sharing of ideas becomes enhanced.

Some junior therapists feel intimidated in the presence of the senior therapist. They compare themselves to the senior therapist and evaluate themselves as wanting. They anticipate that the senior therapist will expect or demand answers or contributions from them and they will disappoint and fail the senior therapist or appear stupid in front of the client. If the therapists are unconcerned with prestige considerations, neither therapist need fear admitting ignorance or error, and each can demonstrate a willingness to learn from the other. This is consonant with Adler's opinion that therapists must not be concerned with their worth. They are there to perform the therapeutic task which is to help the patient, not to increase or diminish their feelings of self-worth. The demonstrated courage of the therapist to admit ignorance or to risk being wrong can serve as a powerful lesson for the patient, since one of the therapeutic objectives is to teach the patient the courage to be imperfect (Lazarsfeld, 1936, 1966). Either therapist can be wrong, misinformed, off the track or noncomprehending, but in an atmosphere of mutual respect, none of these proves an obstacle to therapy. On occasion when one therapist may be making the other uncomfortable, some therapists have devised a prearranged signal which informs the other therapist that the other is becoming uncomfortable.

One situation which makes junior therapists, especially, uncomfortable is one where the senior therapist asks them a question. They may perceive this question as a demand for an answer. Even when it is, the junior therapist is not required to respond with an answer, if one is not readily available. The junior therpist may respond with "Before I venture an opinion, I'd like to have yours" or may confess, "I wish I had an answer to that." At certain times the senior therapist is merely asking a rhetorical question, merely bouncing his question off the other therapist rather than seeking a reply. The senior therapist may ask the question and reply to it in preference to making a flat statement of opinion or a direct interpretation. Often this question has no other aim than to keep the interview a double interview rather than an individual one.

Another problem which may affect the therapy when a senior and junior therapist collaborate is the junior's treatment of the senior as a guru. The junior therapist may then sit at the feet of the senior seeking to lap up wisdom rather than to engage in therapy. From this posture it is easy for the junior therapist to become deferent, to avoid offering opinions. (Pereu, 1977)

Two therapists who work together must become thoroughly acquainted with each other's styles. In this manner they will avoid making demands upon each other which they cannot fulfill. Communications will be facilitated because each is aware of the other's conscious and unconscious cues, much as good bridge players are. Each will ordinarily detect the directions in which the other is heading and the tactics which the other proposes to use at the moment. Post-session reviews, perhaps listening to tapes of the interview, may be helpful to the therapists in coordinating their styles. For therapists comtemplating working together for the first time, it might prove worthwhile for the therapists to meet and negotiate some temporary structure for their relationship and conduct of the interview. As their experience with each other grows, and each learns the style of the other, a natural therapeutic collaboration will emerge.

An important facilitator of collaboration is the therapists' enjoyment of each other. They work better as a team because each is eager to please and be pleased by the other. Moreover, they listen to each other better when they enjoy each other. Choice of a second therapist depends not only upon the direct interests and needs of the patient but also upon how "sympatico" the two therapists are.

The Relationship of each Therapist to the Other vis-a-vis the Patient

A competitive relationship between the therapists, it has been noted, can adversely affect the relationship with the patient. It may foster the alliance of the patient with one of the therapists who may, in turn, reward the patient with his or her favoritism for the patient's good taste in therapists. The patient may be invited to take sides. Patients, especially if they have within their own family constellations played off one parent versus the other, may attempt to re-create this process in the therapeutic interview. For those who conceptualize multiple therapy as a re-creation of the family setting, Lundin & Aronov (1952) offer an additional caution.

> Subtle intrafamily influences in the past have often made him the scapegoat for the unresolved conflicts of his own parents. If now, in group therapy, the patient senses the same lack of respect, the same disharmony and infantile competition which marked his early years, then the basic purpose of the co-therapist method will be lost. The patient will have no recourse but to further strengthen sick defenses which were erected during his childhood. For this reason people who work as co-therapists must be reasonably conscious of their feelings for one another. Systematic evaluations of therapy sessions are extremely important, an honest and open criticism is to be encouraged. (p. 79)

Factors other than competition may also contribute to problems in therapy. Differences in style between the therapists may contribute to the patient's preference for the more directive or less directive therapist, the gentler or more confrontive therapist, the listener therapist or the talker therapist. In some therapies, one therapist may protect the patient from the other therapist when the first therapist regards the second as being too hard on the patient. The first therapist may come to the rescue or defense of patients, neutralize the second therapist's interpretations, and in essence communicate to them that they need not pay much attention to the second therapist. Carried to an extreme they may even fail to schedule regular double interviews. These processes may be set in motion by the patient who may maneuver a vulnerable therapist into this position. When this situation originates with the therapists, one or both therapists may have personal problems which are intruding into their therapeutic work or a conflict of therapeutic philosophies exists. Both conditions merit investigation. In innovative fashion, Levinson (1969) uses his dog as a co-therapist, and similar problems emerge. When using a canine co-therapist,

> The psychotherapist emotionally must be able to surrender part of his functioning as a pet. He must be able to permit the child to use the pet and not to feel slighted because of it. He should have awareness of his own conflicts so as not to intrude them on the children he is treating. The psychotherapist must face the following questions: Does he harbor unconscious sibling rivalry with the pet which may interfere with the treatment? Is he somewhat jealous because the pet is becoming a friend of the child? (p. 183)

We have already in several instances pointed out that the attitudes held or exhibited by any of the participants may derive from either the situation or the life styles of either the therapists or the patient. This represents a general problem in conducting psychotherapy and is not limited to multiple psychotherapy. The problem is, however, accentuated in multiple therapy in much the same manner that it may manifest itself within a family constellation. Just as we do not have a concern ourselves with sibling rivalry or alliances in a one-child family, we do not have to concern ourselves with the competition between therapists in the individual therapy situation. In the context of multiple therapy we must not only examine many more relationships, but we must distinguish between the overt, observable behavior of the participants and their covert, nonconscious motivation and attitudes.

Chapter 7

Supervision and Training Through Multiple Psychotherapy

As mentioned in Chapter 1, Hadden (1947) was the first to describe the use of a co-therapist in group psychotherapy for this purpose. Haigh & Kell were acquainted with Dreikurs' use of multiple psychotherapy as a routine procedure and in their paper (1950) recognized its value in training. Haigh & Kell were involved in training clinical psychologists at the University of Chicago and so had ample opportunity to examine its value as a training tool. Others who have published on the use of multiple psychotherapy in training are Hill & Worden (1952), Lott (1952) and Yalom & Handlon (1966).

Many novice therapists in traditional forms of training see their first patients without ever having witnessed the therapy in operation. Occasionally their sole experience with the therapy is through reading, academic lectures, watching a movie or through being a patient when a "didactic" therapeutic experience is a requirement for the practice of the therapy. Multiple psychotherapy provides opportunities for the student therapist to observe and participate at the same time; to see the patient alone and then together with an instructor; to function under the watchful eye of the instructor and then receive the latter's critique. Thus, not only a better entry to therapy is provided, but also a closer and more cogent supervision. One instructor can supervise a half-dozen students and one student can have a half-dozen instructors or a half-dozen different cases.

Reassurance and Support in Supervision

When multiple psychotherapy provides the framework for training, the trainee can observe and participate and simultaneously be observed and supervised. The instructor can provide immediate assistance to the trainee if needed. He can take control of a floundering interview, re-channel it to avoid impasses and can introduce new tactics. He can encourage the trainee to plough ahead knowing that the instructor will help and guide him.

In a completely open arrangement, the patient can know and accept the trainee *qua* trainee and can also be assured that the instructor guards his welfare as well as that of the trainee. Sometimes the patient imitates the instructor and helps and encourages the trainee. By treating the trainee with respect, he not only encourages him, but also elevates him to respectful status in the eyes of the patient.

In short, both instructor and trainee play a dual role. The instructor is both teacher and therapist. Both patient and trainee are his responsibility and his goal is to foster a working therapeutic relationship between the other two. His method of teaching is almost never didactic during the double interview itself. He must learn to ask questions which elicit answers rather than supplying them himself, to provide a number of possible interpretations from which trainee and patient may select the most appropriate rather than mention the appropriate interpretation only. Instead of making *dicta*, he may wonder aloud if something "could be." Just as the experienced therapist encourages the patient to discover his own interpretations, so does the instructor encourage the trainee to try his own interpretations. The instructor thus orchestrates and conducts.

The trainee is both therapist and student. He also is responsible to patient and instructor; to the former, to help, to the latter to learn. The more he learns, the more he can help. His job is to display his wares so that the instructor can view them and integrate them into the orchestration of the therapeutic encounter.

A brief session between the instructor and trainee after the double interview is invaluable. The trainee can ask the instructor to explain each of his interventions and his own thoughts and share with the instructor what took place in his own head. This is on-the-job training indeed, with the apprentice directly learning the skills of the master.

Acquisition of Skills

Thus, learning skills occurs in several ways in multiple therapy: (1) observation and imitation, (2) discussion with and feedback from the instructor, and (3) practicing the skills in the presence of the instructor.

All of the instructor's skills are hopefully modeled for the student. Each double interview models how to begin and terminate an interview, how to sift through verbiage to reach the core of an issue, how to respond to expressions of feeling, how to interpret and how to accept, respect and encourage the patient. A wide range of cases will offer numerous other model situations: how to deal with hostility, silence, discouragement, symptom litanies, complaints and even touchy situations such as a possible suicide.

Becoming skilled requires time as well as training and experience. The tyro can expect to be much more knowledgeable after 10 cases than after two. In multiple therapy this skill acquisition can be expected to proceed much faster.

Le Fevre (1977), speaking from the vantage point of a trainee, found several benefits in multiple psychotherapy which accrue to the trainee: less anxiety for the trainee, gradual increase in participation as confidence grows, learning one's limitations quickly, learning to survive mistakes and recover from them, learning to accept imperfections without being defensive about them and a faster rate of learning. She experienced a sense of high involvement and of shared responsibility. Having the freedom both to participate and to observe, she reported that she became more sensitive to her own emotional reactions to different patients and learned to express these feelings in a therapeutic way. She observed different kinds of therapeutic interventions such as humor, exaggeration, confrontation and support and how to use them. She was forced to learn to deal openly with problems in the therapeutic relationship since the instructor brought them up openly. She found after-sessions with the instructor useful for discussing any questions that she still had after the double session. She concludes that she cannot imagine a more effective mode of training than multiple psychotherapy, stating that it enabled her to feel like an effective therapist in a very short time with minimal anxiety and maximal freedom to be herself in the therapeutic relationship.

Observation and Participation

Le Fevre, as already stated, appreciated the chance to be both observer and participant. The supervisor can also play both roles. Each is able to remain passive and watch the therapeutic interaction between the other two.

For supervisors, it permits observation of the trainees in action and yet permits them to intervene as they deem necessary or desirable. For trainees, it becomes possible to withdraw when they are unsure or when they wish to observe what the supervisor is doing. As time progresses, trainees may prove willing to assume greater risk and responsibility, especially as they perceive their supervisors as nonthreatening. Trainees relax, venture forth with less caution and increasing confidence and with the knowledge that both they and the patient will likely succeed.

Supervisors must know when to observe and when to participate. Very active supervisors may "take over" too much and conduct individual therapy with the patient while the trainee just watches. The double interview requires active participation by both therapists in an atmosphere of free and open interchange of views. The responsibility is shared. The supervisor will intervene to comment, suggest, guide and explain, but unless he spends some time just observing, he will not be able to see the trainee at work. Furthermore, because trainees may be reluctant to expose themselves by participating, it is incumbent upon the supervisor to draw in the trainee with questions which require the trainee to give his opinions, make interpretations and express feelings. Instead of "solving" problems himself, the supervisor encourages both trainee and patient to participate by asking for suggestions about how to proceed.

Learning Therapeutic Styles

A peril inherent in such supervision is that trainees may begin to mimic their supervisors. Even when they share the same theoretical background, different therapists have different styles and employ different tactics and strategies with different patients. While experienced therapists resemble each other in their approaches (Fiedler, 1950), they nevertheless exhibit different modes in their conduct of psychotherapy and in the kinds of relationships they establish with patients. When trainees work in multiple psychotherapy with several supervisors they can witness several styles of therapist behavior. They discover that there is no "one right way" to do therapy, no rigid set of rules; but that effective psychotherapy can take different forms. Each supervisor will have a different personality and will use it in a different way. Each supervisor will display a different armamentarium of tactics, strategies and devices. Each supervisor will relate to the trainee in a different way. This melange of methods helps the trainee to select what is comfortable for him. The trainee, hopefully, learns not to merely imitate, but to make tactics, strategies and devices of his own and use his own uniqueness therapeutically.

Learning About Oneself

Mosak (1950) has pointed out "therapy is a two-way street." Therefore, while "our emphasis in therapy has consisted of examining *what the therapist did* and *what happened to the patient,*" Mosak observes that "the therapist also has the responsibility to observe *himself* in the course of therapy." Experiencing oneself and learning about oneself, while occurring in individual psychotherapy, are intensified in multiple therapy since the trainee is not actively involved at every moment. It is probably easier for the trainee to become aware of what he does and does not know, of what he still has to learn.

In addition, a time-honored aspect of psychotherapy supervision has included the concept that the supervisor observes not only the trainee's technical behavior but also those aspects of personality that may interfere with the therapeutic relationship. Thus, the supervisor, either during the double session or later, points out to the trainee the behavior which interfered with therapy and makes inferences about possible personality traits that lead to this behavior; e.g., that the trainee becomes too anxious at the patient's expression of a dysphoric feeling and hastens to comfort so quickly that the patient inhibits further expression of the feeling; or, that the trainee has become defensive when criticized. In the first case, the supervisor might infer that the trainee becomes too uncomfortable in the presence of suffering; in the second case, that he overprotects himself and his image of competence.

Not all teachers of psychotherapy are so enthusiastic about using it for training. Indeed, Haley (1973) specifically objects to the technique. He prefers to have the supervisor watch through a one-way mirror. When the supervisor wants to in-

tervene, he calls the trainee on the telephone and makes suggestions. Supervisors have their own personal preferences for
various methods. We prefer multiple psychotherapy.

Chapter 8
A Life Style Formulation Interview

In Chapter 3 we briefly described our favorite method for introducing the patient to multiple psychotherapy: after the initial meeting with one therapist, the patient is asked to see the other therapist for a structured interview (which may take from one to three sessions). At this time the second therapist gathers information about the patient's childhood for the specific purpose of bringing this information, in organized form, to a double session at which both therapists will be present. At times, it will be simpler for the first therapist to collect this information, in which case the double session will be the first meeting between the patient and second therapist. The structure of the data collection may be discovered from a perusal of the Life Style Inventory (Mosak and Shulman, 1971). See Appendix II.

The method of collecting this childhood information has been described in detail many times Dreikurs, (1954); Shulman (1962); Mosak (1958); MeKelvie and Friedland (1978). When the data-collecting therapist presents the material to the other therapist at the double session, he does so in organized fashion so that the listening therapist can begin to organize his formulation of what Adlerians call the Life Style. The double session is thus highly structured. The following segment is part of such a Life Style formulation session, the formulation of a summary of the family constellation.

The segment shows the interplay and cooperation between the therapists as well as the participation of the patient. C stands for consultant, T for therapist and P for patient.

A Life Style Formulation Session

T-1 P came here because he is (and I use his words) "homosexually-oriented." He didn't want to be a homosexual but until recently he felt that homosexuals were born and, therefore, he was stuck with it.

C-1 Mm-hm.

T-2 So, that's what he comes for. In his sibling constellation there is Alice, 5; Mort, ten months, and then, P, who is 27 years old. Now, father had a son from a previous marriage, Paul, whom P did not know about until P was in the seventh grade, so he was about 12 years old before he knew that Paul was a homosexual. Paul prevailed upon both Mort and P to engage in homosexual relations . . . it was, and perhaps still is a puzzle to P that Mort did not become homosexually-oriented.

Alice was at the top of the class . . . but, she was socially backward. She was quiet, nice-looking, warm . . . she got along well with P and they were affectionate with each other and could talk to each other.

Of Mort, he says, "we were like twins. People thought we were twins." He was the dull one . . . he had a tough time in school. However, he was athletic . . . he liked sports. He got into trouble making mischief and playing pranks. Mort and P were inseparable . . . they even shared the same baby carriage. It changed, however, when they got to school and each developed his own friendships. Mort and P, he later said, had "pee" contests to see who could pee the farthest. (We were talking about the concept of masculinity and what boys do and he said, "Yeh, come to

T-1 In this session consultant is seeing P for the first time. T has done the intake and collected the material for the formulation.

T-2 Describing the sibling constellation, P is the youngest, following closely on the heels of another boy. Each sibling will be described as will P himself.

T-2 The information that P and Mort were inseparable until school started will crop up again later.

58

think of it, Mort and I did have pee contests.")

C-2   See who would stand farthest away from the wall and still hit the wall?

T-3   Yeh, uh huh, that kind of thing. P felt Mort didn't like him because P was so smart. Mort would bang his head in frustration on the floor because P could do something and Mort couldn't. "I was a little shit . . . I was terrible . . . I was always bright . . . no one could tell me anything. I would have tantrums and mother would stick my head under the cold water faucet. I was funny . . . I kept the house in a constant uproar. The room was always focused on me." When P went to school and changed, he went the other way. At school he was the model, the top of his class, too, just like his sister and he got even quieter when he went to high school.

So, there were the three of them, until he was about twelve years old, and in comes Paul, the long-lost son. Paul had been raised by the maternal grandmother. He was homosexual and he came to live with the family and introduced both boys to homosexual acts.

T-4   P liked it but he didn't want to . . . he despised Paul. P was always fighting with him trying to upset things so that maybe Paul would get so upset and angry that he would leave the house permanently.

C-3   P felt . . . like, get rid of Paul and I can solve the problem?

T-5   Yeh . . . however, people did not understand his motivation and they thought that he was a "son of a bitch" for his attitude towards his brother.

C-4   O.K.

T-3   P played the role of family attention-getter, a role that fits in with his ambition to be the "star" which will be mentioned later.

59

T-6 Mort was sort of the dumb one and P was the super bright one. Mort was athletic ... P was non-athletic.

Alice was most like P. "We cried a lot ... we were so good and why did we get dumped on ... we were two suffering saints." Alice and P played together, although before school, P and Mort were inseparable. Who fought? ... P fought with everybody.

P doesn't relate any childhood fears; however, his childhood ambition was to be a star of stage, screen, Broadway, and everything.

C-5 To be a star ...

T-7 But a total star ... In terms of the ratings from most to least ... intelligence Alice, P ... grades ... Alice and P got straight A's. Industrious ... Alice, P, Mort. Alice had the highest standards of achievement. Athletic ... Mort, P., Alice. Daring ... Mort, P, Alice. Looks ... Alice was pretty ... then P, then Mort.

C-6 Is there any change in that order ... all the way through the ratings?

T-8 Uh ...

C-7 Since Mort obviously represents one pole, Alice the other.

T-9 Yes, yes! Yes! It changes somewhat in the social area. Alice was the most feminine, Mort was the most masculine. Alice was the most obedient. P was also obedient but, he answered back. Made mischief ... Mort, P. Alice. Mort was openly rebellious, P was covertly rebellious ... He did what he was supposed to, but he hated it. P was the most punished for answering back.

C-8 Oh, P was the most punished?

T-10 Yeh! He had a 'big mouth.' The highest standards of right and wrong ... ?

T-6 Rating the siblings against each other on various traits or observable behavior is part of the material used for the formulation. The interrelationships between the siblings is also used.

T-7 These are comparative ratings. Thus Alice was most industrious, Mort was the least.

C-7 Note that C has already found consistency in the ratings.

Alice, Mort. Critical of others . . . P,
Alice, Mort. Critical of self . . . Mort,
followed by Alice and P, equally. Mort
was the most easy-going, then Alice,
then P.

C-9   Mort was the most easy-going, but was the most critical of self?

C-9   Any apparent discrepancy in the information must be investigated.

T-11 He did whatever the hell, he wanted to! But he also was frustrated with these two straight A students there and would bang his head against the wall.

C-10 Would it be correct to say Mort was the least fussy?

P-1   Yes.

P-1   Up to now, P has been a listener. Now he offers to participate.

T-12 Yes. It would be . . . that comes later. Charm and the desire to please were both P's.

C-11 Not Alice?

T-13 No, she was socially backward.

C-12 Oh! go on . . .

T-14 Most cheerful . . . Mort, Alice, P. The most sociable . . . Mort, P, Alice. The sense of humor . . . P. Considerate . . . Alice, P. Mort. P, the most bossy . . . P demanded his way. Nobody got his way. P had a temper. P was the fighter . . . P had a chip on his shoulder. P sulked . . . P was stubborn. Alice was shy . . . followed by P and Mort. Mort and Alice were sensitive and easily hurt. P was idealistic. In terms of materialism, P liked nice things . . . still does. Methodical and neat . . . P, Alice, Mort. Responsible . . . Alice, P., Mort, Alice was withdrawn . . . the two boys were excitement seekers. With respect to physical development, P was small. He was self-conscious about it. He just wanted to be big because big people were more attractive, in being sought after for friendship.

T-14 These trait ratings will be used to understand the coping styles of each sibling, their areas of success and failure and some aspects of their interpersonal relationships.

C-13 So, it was a status symbol?

T-15 Mm Hm!

T-16 School information . . . Alice was a hard
act to follow. P wasn't jealous of her . . .
he thought she was wonderful. He liked English, Art, and Music . . . He did
not like recess because he had to perform in sports and "I didn't want to,
because I didn't do it right!"

C-14 Didn't do it right?

T-17 "I threw a baseball like a girl does" was
his answer to the question about not
doing it right. Social information . . .
He had a lot of friends. He played with
the girls too much and was considered
a sissy, and he felt crummy because of
this, so he stopped playing with the
girls.

T-17 This is both a critical
remark and a form of
self-identification. It is
consistent with his
self image as a
homosexual and his
unhappiness with this
self image.

C-15 Let me review before you go on . . . He
did not want to play ball at recess
because he threw like a girl . . .

T-18 Uh, Huh.

C-16 He stopped playing with girls because
they considered him a sissy for playing
with the girls?

P-2 I think the girls would still let me play
with them but I . . . well, I played with
the girls a lot really pre-school and the
very first grades and then, because
society told me not to, then I stopped
playing with the girls, too.

P-2 Participates to clarify.
In a double interview
of this type, it is usual
for the P to listen in-
tently to the informa-
tion about himself as
P is doing. Never-
theless, P is often en-
couraged to amend or
clarify.

C-17 But you stopped because . . .

P-3 I wasn't supposed to.

C-18 Because you weren't supposed to.

P-4 Yes.

C-19 Uh, the implication seems to be that
along about this time you are feeling
about yourself, that you are not
masculine as Mort . . .

P-5 Yes.

T-19 You can also see from this he is still
concerned with status . . . Earlier when
we talked about physical
developments, smallness deprives him

of social status and here being a sissy deprives him of social status.

C-20 You know, it seems as if masculinity itself is treated as a status symbol.

C-20 This interchange between C & T allows P to follow the reasoning of the other two. Almost all patients listen reflectively and attentively when the two therapists talk about them.

T-20 Mm, Hm ... and being an attention getter is also. He wants to be the star of stage, TV, Broadway, etc., he wants positive attention. He doesn't want the negative attention Mort got, so therefore, if something brings negative attention, then to hell with it.

T-20 T agrees and adds that attention also gives status for P.

C-21 Simply avoid those things you don't do well or ...

T-21 Look well at ...

C-22 Or those areas where you don't make good impression.

P-6 Right

P-6 These observations by P corroborate the interpretations of the therapists.

C-23 You concentrate where you do make a good impression ... and it seems to happen the same way to Mort, too. Mort apparently gave up where he felt he wasn't as good as the others. P apparently gave up in athletics because he wasn't as good as Mort.

T-22 But you also see even the way P handled school versus home. At home he got positive attention for being the comedian, etc., he was the comedian, and at school where he got positive attention for being a model student, he became a model student and avoided being a comedian.

T-22 Since T and C are trying to formulate personality structure and dynamics they look for consistencies, and even how consistent traits are differentially expressed in different situations.

C-24 Yeh! So that, P, you went wherever the payoff was.

P-7 Right!

T-23 And the payoff is in social terms ... not as much winning, as stardom. Now, P didn't want to play with the kids. He would rather be down at the office where his father worked and he would go down to the office and work with father, or for him and sometimes as early as age nine, he ran father's office . . . and he would make out the bills and greet the customers and do all the things there. Father would even leave the office and leave P in charge.

"I thought I was a big deal! People would say to my father, "Is that your kid working for you . . . Or is that a midget?" And father would burst with pride. But, there again, you see the positive attention accruing to him so, as you said, he went where the payoff was. There was more payoff at the office than there was playing with the other kids, especially in sports,

Sexual information? . . . Mother told him that when he was born grandmother had said she had never seen such a small, cute penis, and that on that basis he would become a priest.

I had the same look on my face (laughter) . . .

C-25 I don't really know how to take that . . . (laughter) . . .

T-24 His sex information came from mother in small doses. He does not know why father would not tell him anything about sex.

C-26 Uh Huh!

T-25 There was some sex exploration before he went to school and one girl laughed because his was so small.

C-27 I guess this is another area in which size is status.

T-26 Size is status. But at any rate, you could well imagine that somebody who is concerned with how other people think about him and react to him, isn't

T-23 T responds to the look on C's face.

C-25 The laughter is good natured of course and P joined in.

C-27 The main issue for this patient is his competitive aspiration for high status in all areas. Masculinity and its attendant at-

64

going to take a very small penis out and display it to the world.

C-28 I can see that.

P-8 It was embarrassing in a lot of places, like in the service, in college, etc. I avoided locker rooms.

C-29 Would anybody make remarks about it?

P-9 Well, not in the service . . . It's really funny . . . ! People were kinda gentlemanly!

C-30 How about college?
College people would make cracks?

P-10 Uh, when uh, my roommate did once . . . that's all . . . the one time . . . it embarrassed the hell out of me!

C-31 O.K. let's go on.

T-27 Father was very strict. He didn't seem to have too much of a sense of humor. He always wanted to stop the laughing . . . the humor. At the same time he was a practical joker, but I thought he was very good. He was smart but not cultured . . . You couldn't speak back to Father, but you could speak back to mother. If P had negative feelings toward Father, he would avoid father because when father got mad at him it hurt. "He was very frugal . . . you couldn't get any money out of daddy." Mort was his favorite because Mort was like Father. Mort reminded Father of what he was like when he was a kid. His ambitions for the children . . . for Alice to go a lot farther, to be the real educated one. P doesn't remember any ambitions being held out for the boys. P was a disappointment to him. "I was different. I was not interested in sports." "He wishes I were more like Mort. He was proud of my marks."
Mort was most like Father but "Mort complained about him just like I did."

tributes is simply another area in which to achieve status. It is not surprising that he questions his masculinity since he feels low status in that area.

T-27 Description of the parents is important information for the life style formulation.

65

Mother was a housewife. She was very warm ... and she appreciated beautiful things like music and reading books. She had a good vocabulary. She wrote all the letters in the family, even to Father's mother. She only had a high school education ... but ... she painted and did things like that!

"She was a sloppy housekeeper although she didn't think she was ... but we all did! She had a temper ... flew off the handle easily, but was easy to make up with afterward. She was the storyteller. She was dramatic ... felt sorry for herself a lot." She complained that father was mean, that everyone took the spotlight from her. She felt that she was the ugliest, most untalented in her family. Still, at the same time, there were times when mother boasted she had the prettiest kids in the whole family.

C-32 Mother dealt in superlatives.

T-28 Mm, Hm!

Mother's favorite? "I was. She planned on it before I was born" ... and it was here he related that grandmother built up the story before P was born that he would be a wonder baby ... he would be the one to stick by her.

C-33 Stick by whom? ... Mother or Grandmother?

T-29 By Mother. He says "I was the big accident I discovered later in life" ... Mother had not planned to have two children within ten months.

C-34 Oh!

T-30 And when she felt bad, Grandmother ... tried to make her feel better ... this will be the *wunderkind!* Ambitions for the children? She wanted Alice to go to college. P doesn't know what she wanted him to be. She wanted Mort to

T-30 This description of a parent is an example of how the material is reviewed by T and C. T uses verbatum

66

be just happy, which he was not. Her relationship with her children? She taught us how to play, to work puzzles, to draw, to cut out and all that kind of stuff. P is most like Mother, interested in art, music, and all pretty things. Parent's relationship? Mother was kind of dependent on father ... she hid behind his strength. Mother didn't handle the kitchen, the checkbook or grocery shopping. He wanted all the responsibilities and she was willing to let him have it. She didn't handle anybody. The parents were openly affectionate; still, they fought a lot. They fought about Grandmother, about money ... Mother wanted something and Father would say almost automatically he couldn't afford it! They fought about a lot of things which P considered to be trivial ... like the housekeeping. They were a poor family ... they did not have a lot of things others kids had. They had a raggedy house. Additional parental figures? ... There was a maternal grandmother already mentioned "who would come to see us. She was a beautiful lady with snow white hair. She was nice to sit on and cuddle ... very loving ... she smelled good. I was her favorite because I kept her in stitches. I could tell her "Go home, Grandma" and she would bust out laughing! But, if Mort were to say to her, "Why don't you go home, Grandma?" she would feel insulted and might just go home" ... so that he could get away with much more than Mort could with grandma.

C-35 Let's try to summarize this material. This will just be a summary, P, hitting the high points and in your discussion

statements made by P.

C-35 The recital of information is complete and C will try to summarize.

67

with T the two of you can fill in the framework. Let's all try to do this together. P, if you feel that our interpretation may be wrong, please interrupt and help us get it right.

T-31 Or, if you want to add something which occurs to you! . . .

P11 O.K.

C-36 Now, he's actually the youngest of three for . . . our purposes . . . in a family which is divided into father and Mort, in one group, and mother, Alice, and P, in another in terms of disposition-personality type. He and Mort each discouraged the other since apparently each was competitive and wanted to perform only when assured of success. If you disagree with that, please tell us.

P-12 I very much agree with that. I'm still doing that now.

C-37 O.K. Therefore, Mort was discouraged academically while P was discouraged in the so-called masculine pursuit . . . those that he felt would have obtained father's approval. I'd like to point out in an aside, here, that P gives evidence that father did approve of him. Father was proud of him when he worked in the office . . . and of his academic achievement and, yet, P feels Mort was his favorite . . . "I was a disappointment because I wasn't good in sports." But Mort was as much a disappointment because he didn't do well in school.

T-32 Or because he misbehaved.

C-38 Yeh! . . . or whatever it is . . . so that your earlier statement, T, that P wanted to be a total star could easily lead P to be much more aware of the areas in which he failed than of the areas in which he did please father.

P is now invited to participate.

C-36 Birth order is considered an important factor by Adlerians in a person's early life situation. The marked division of areas of endeavor between Mort and P is considered evidence of competition for status among the siblings.

C-38 This interpretive statement highlights P's tendency to pay more attention to failure, to be perhaps more motivated by a

68

P-13 I think that ... well ... I think I always knew it. I used to always test myself to see if I really could ... uh ... uh ... do things as well as Mort. I ... Mort could never catch ... If I were pulling a prank or something, fighting with Mort, and I started to run, he could never catch me. I was faster than he was. And, uh, I remember mother and father going to the movies on Tuesday night when they got "dish night" so that they could be gone, you know, every Tuesday, so, you know, for a week we'd plan what kind of an attack we were gonna have with Mort, see ... My sister might have been baby-sitting and we would, you know ... run all around the house 'n, uh, ... it's fantastic but ... the stuff we'd do! I remember one night we called a truce at twenty minutes to ten to clean the spaghetti off the walls because Mother and Dad were coming back. We had a great time together when we were alone and then I was just as good as he was ... you know, I could catch him ...

C-39 Mm ...

P-14 In these games together ... there were no rules, see ... to these games.

C-40 Uh huh!

P-15 And, uh, that was the time I really felt that Mort and I were really friends ...

C-41 Mm Hm!

P-16 And then, of course, the next day at school, Mort didn't want to have anything to do with me. Because I was ...

C-42 The statement that was made was that you and Mort would be inseparable until you started school and then each developed his own friends.

P-17 Right, right!

fear of failure than by a desire for achievement.

P-13 P distinguishes between behavior intended for the parental audience and behavior intended to prove to himself his own competence vis-a-vis Mort.

C-43 What you seem to be saying is that other people broke up a beautiful friendship between you and Mort . . .

P-28 Yes.

C-44 And if only . . .

T-33 They'd let us alone . . .

C-45 Yeh . . . or, if only one didn't have to take other people into account.

P-18 Or on vacation . . . we had a ball on vacation because there was nobody else to take him away from me.

P-18 The patient is always permitted to elaborate on the interpretation. P takes an active part in interpreting the family constellation.

C-46 It looks to us like uh . . . uh . . . you were very good friends when there was no audience around to play to . . . and that once, uh, the audience was involved the rule was that all's fair in love, war, and on stage.

P-19 Yes!

C-47 Now, father was seen as a distant authoritarian, fearful judge, who was the power in the family. P felt less able to influence father . . .

C-47 C resumes the summary.

P-20 Yeh!

C-48 than anyone else . . .

P-21 Right!

C-49 And, therefore, his approval was the most important of all! All the approval you got from mother or the other people really didn't count as much as father's approval would have.

P-22 Mother's was so easy to get . . . (Pause)

C-50 What are you saying, P? The harder to get it is, the more it's worth?

P-23 Yeh!

C-51 Spoken like a true competitor (chuckle).

T-34 He's made the same statement about his grades. Since he didn't work hard for them, he doesn't really know how much they're worth.

T-34 Note how T supports C's interpretation. This is an example of the teamwork between the two therapists.

C-52 Right! True achievement seems based more upon effort and risk than it is upon simple accomplishment.

P-24 Yeh!

C-53 It isn't what you accomplish; it's how much you had to put in it and how hard you had to work and what the odds were against it . . . that's the real victory for the competitor. That's . . . uh . . . you value the tough audience much more than the easy audience.
Now, mother was an emotional, weaker, yet interested in the niceties of life, who also wanted to be a star.

C-53 C points out another important value for P. True achievement requires heroism and triumph. P is more attracted to challenges rather than to easy gains.

T-35 Uh . . . we haven't yet said that he wanted to be a star.

T-35 T helps C to formulate the summary.

C-54 All right . . . who wanted to be a star and used techniques of dramatization, sensitivity and suffering.

P-25 When you say she wants to be a star, does that mean she wanted to be a great achiever or . . .

T-36 Somebody who wants to be noticed.

P-26 Noticed . . . O.K. . . . I'll buy that!

C-55 Yeh! The, uh, . . . not bothering with the housework but paying more attention to the music or to the painting. See, you became interested in achievement because it was one of the ways that you could be a star . . . but, if charm did it, then you would do it that way, too.

C-55 Adlerians typically see the underlying source trait as the consistent aspect of personality. The surface behavior changes with the environmental contingency.

T-37 And if uproar did it . . .

C-56 Yeh! Yeh! . . . Or, if suffering did it!

T-38 He describes himself as a suffering saint.

C-57 O.K. . . . so that the role that you play is less important than the stardom that it achieves.

T-39 Somebody said to the critic whatever you say about me, good or bad, just be sure you spell my name right.

T-39 Elaborating statements help explain and confirm the interpretation.

71

C-58 Because that is the interest of the star.

C-59 Now let's say P found his place as the indulged and pampered mother's youngest son.

T-40 Can I change a word?

C-60 Yeh!

T-41 Wunderkind! He was not only a son.

C-61 Destined to be something special . . . a source of great joy . . .

P-27 It wasn't always a joy.

P-27 P feels free to disagree. C accepts P's statement.

C-62 Well, something special . . . even when you weren't a great joy, you were something special. He basked in this attention and competed for it in all ways that worked . . . academic success, charm, temper . . .

T-42 Being a comedian?

C-63 Yeh! Cuteness . . . and avoided all of the techinques that did not pay off or made him look second best.

T-43 Or foolish!

C-64 Yeh! hm . . . He felt least apt in those qualities most shown by Mort . . . which in his mind became associated with masculinity. Therefore, he did not feel he could star as a male.

C-64 C compares the goal of being a star to P's feeling about his own masculinity.

Chapter 9
When Therapy Bogs Down

The following interview shows one of the most useful aspects of multiple psychotherapy. In the case of this patient, therapy has bogged down into a series of unproductive interviews in which the patient repeatedly reports his failures, his mistakes, and his poor judgment. The therapist interprets the behavior and the patient accepts them, but nothing changes. At this point, the consultant, who has not seen the patient for two months, is called in.

The consultant is able to bring a new focus into the therapy — he interprets the patient's intentions and invites the patient to pursue his goal openly, one form of the technique which Wexberg called counter-suggestion and Frankl called paradoxical intention.

The interview protocol shows how a teasing humor can sometimes be used to reveal the patient's own goals to him.

All of these participants are male. The consultant is a senior and more experienced therapist. C stands for consultant, T for therapist and P for patient.

C-1 Now let's hear about P.

C-1 In this double interview, the consultant (in this case the senior author) addresses himself sometimes to the patient about the last few interviews, sometimes to the therapist. Here the opening question leaves it up to either who wishes to answer. In this case the patient does.

P-1 Everything is worse. To sum it up briefly, I am not getting my Masters, I am about to lose my job and to break up with my girlfriend.

C-2 Yes.

P-2 And I've spent almost all the money that I had saved up very recklessly on an automobile that I didn't need.

C-3 (laugh) Isn't it wonderful how he brags about how badly he is doing?

T-1 Yes. We talked a little bit about that last time.

C-4 Everything goes wrong, but he tells it with a smile. As if he would say, "Look what a bad boy I am!"

T-2 He shows off his inadequacy.

C-5 And he tries to prove to us how bad he is.

C-3 This is an attempt to interpret to the patient the meaning of his remarks; it emphasizes and exaggerates the absurdity of his attitude and is directed to the other therapist who responds. The discussion emphasizes the patient's goals, the purpose of his actions or feelings. The patient, listening in, becomes more aware of what he is doing than if the interpretation were given to him directly and perhaps provoke defensive attitudes. Whenever the patient feels either misunderstood, has a question, or "catches on," he speaks up.

T-3 Yes, he succeeds in doing that. We brought up the topic why he should have done such things. It seems as if he wanted to show the world how much of a baby he is, and how he can't be trusted to take care of himself. Naturally, then, others will take care of him.

C-6 But there seems to be something else in his description of his activities. Ap-

T-3 This interpretation refers to the life style, established in earlier sessions.

C-6 Here attention is focused on the present

parently, P came to a point where it is difficult for him to decide what to do with his life. It seems that in order to move in the right direction he would have to be courageous, to believe in his own strength – but that he does only in his fantasies, where he pictures himself as being important. It looks to me as if he would right now pile up explosives to have a good blow up, with the hope that after the explosion he might be thrown to some quiet and secure place. People behave sometimes in this way when they are in a tight spot. Then, whatever comes – it is not their responsibility. We may even find a certain kind of adventurous eagerness to see what will happen when everything blows up.

P-3 You have described it very well. It just seems that no matter where I turn now, I will fail, that no matter what I will do, I'll make it worse for myself.

C-7 So let's see what happens when things will blow up.

P-4 But I . . . uh . . .

T-4 It sounds like getting out of the house by pulling the house down on top of you.

C-8 That's right.

P-5 Yes, exactly.

C-9 But we watch it. It is very interesting.

P-6 The thing is, I don't want it to happen.

situation. The interpretation is partly based on the initial statement of the patient, partly on the development observed in previous interviews. The key interpretation is given at this time – that it is P's intention to create an explosion.

P-3 It is obvious that the patient's passivity during the discussion was fruitful. Here he injects himself, recapitulating what he has understood.

T-4 When the patient hesitates, the second therapist steps in; here he continues the interpretation.

P-5 Again, the patient's attentiveness is demonstrated.

P-6 We can see how the patient integrates what he heard. First, he was impressed with the validity of the interpretation. Now he grasps the full meaning. He begins to de-

C-10 Excuse me, did I hear right. You have just proven to us how you do everything possible to make things worse.

C-10 As soon as he switches to the assumption of his innocence, almost refuting what he admitted before, he is immediately checked. The slight irony, which goes through the whole interview, and which is in line with the tone that the patient set at the beginning is used to be impressive. Some dramatic remark like this saves many sentences of explanation.

T-5 C, may I fill in a little bit? I can give you the trigger mechanism of this particular state of depression in which P seems to be. He was feeling pretty confident. He has some success with Emily. He felt somewhat depressed after a quarrel, but he completed his studies until the only thing that stood between him and his degree was one final examination. He started off all right, but as soon as he came to the first question that he could not answer, he gave up and did not finish the final test.

T-5 The therapist steps in, both to take the pressure off the patient and to deal in an explanatory way with the total situation. His remarks indicate his sensitivity in sizing up the trend of the interview. It changes the tone and the atmosphere. As the patient begins to doubt that he really prompts what is happening, the therapist tries to explain in a calm and objective way how the patient came to this present trend of action.

C-11 As soon as he thinks he is no good, he becomes no good.

fend himself against the impact.

T-6 And so he flunked the exam.

C-12 And is there no chance of taking it again?

P-7 Yes, I can take it next summer if I want to, but . . .

T-7 Yes, but what?

P-8 I want to take it, of course, as it stands, but there is so much uncertainty. Maybe I'm no good and never will succeed as a social worker. Maybe I should look for work in some other field.

T-7 The therapist maintains his active participation so that the discussion remains, for a while, a three-way affair.

C-13 Yes, what field would interest you?

P-9 Uh – the field that would interest me is one that I could never really get into. I would like to be an opera singer, if I had the voice.

T-8 P toys with the idea of doing something other than academic work.

T-8 When the consultant has not seen the patient for a few interviews, then whenever the patient brings up a new point, the therapist relates its significance to the consultant.

C-14 Has he a voice?

T-9 He has no intention whatsoever of going into any other field except social work.

T-9 Again, the therapist fills in the consultant. This is a lead-in for T-10.

C-15 But why does he think about opera singing? Has he a voice?

T-10 Not at all. You see, every time you ask him, "What would you like to do?" he says, "Well, of course, what I would like to do is impossible." He says maybe he should not be a social worker, but he actually never once thought about something else. I remember once he said, "I should be an elevator operator for $30 a week."

C-16 I wonder why he is thinking about being an elevator operator. He is handsome and good-looking, maybe he was

C-16 A deliberately provocative statement.

thinking about all the girls in the
building who would flirt with him.

P10 I am no longer interested in women.

C-17 (surprised) What happened?

P-11 That's one way in which I have
changed.

P-10 As soon as the patient
disagreed, he spoke
up. This indicates that
his silence during the
preceeding discussion
probably meant in-
terest and agreement.

C-18 How come? What happened? What's
wrong with women all of a sudden?

T-11 He had a success.

C-19 How is that possible? How can a complete failure like you succeed with
Emily?

C-18 C continues to tease.

C-19 The consultant did not
follow up the state-
ment about the pa-
tient's loss of interest
in women by trying to
find out how he felt
and why. That would
be the topic of an en-
suing exploratory
single interview. Here
it seems more impor-
tant to follow up the
main line of the issue
at hand, namely
asssumption of the pa-
tient that he is a
failure.

P-12 That's what I am afraid of now. That
I will do something . . . (all talk at once).

T-12 Oh, he has to ruin again what he has
not spoiled yet.

C-20 See how you fool yourself, P? You say,
"I am afraid of" instead of saying, "I am
considering spoiling that, too." To admit that would be too much for your
conscience; so you say you are afraid of
it. It seems that you may have a good
reason to spoil this relationship, too.
Then you may be free, then you can
leave the country and go to a faraway

P-12 The patient's response
indicates the correct-
ness of the above
emphasis.

C-20 An attempt to explain
to the patient his
private logic.

78

place, an island or something like that, and then you can start all over again.

T-13 No, I don't think that P can go away on his own. It seems that he needs people round him to do things for him.

C-21 I'm not quite sure what he really had in mind. What do you think, P? If worse comes to worse, what will happen to you?

C-21 From here on, the discussion turns to an elaboration of the patient's conscious intentions and plans. All support the assumption of his trying to blow up everything.

P-13 Well, I've been . . . although, I don't take it seriously – but I've been considering some painless way of doing away with myself.

P-13 P confirms C's interpretation that P wants "to go to a faraway place."

C-22 Like what?

P-14 It seems that I am in a situation now that there is just no way out. My parents would be better off drawing my insurance than they would be having me, as things stand now.

C-23 That is true for many men on whom others depend.

P-15 If they . . . if they . . . if I am unable to find a job, that is. And it seems that any time I go to interview an employer now, I am going to do something to spoil my prospects of getting that job. I realize that I am going to do that.

P-15 The patient begins to understand his intentions. This kind of insight does not imply cure; but it is an important step toward eventual re-orientation.

C-24 When will you lose your present job?

P-16 They are looking for a replacement for me. As soon as they find it, I will be out. That might be in a month or so.

C-25 And what kind of a job do you consider applying for?

P-17 I know what I want.

C-26 What is it?

P-18 I want a job that would pay $300 a week, at least, and give me enough time for study.

C-27 And what kind of job of this nature is available?

P-19 None that I know of. I know I am setting impossible standards for myself. I would like to find something in case work, but I can't work full time. And jobs which I could get don't pay me enough.

P-19 P creates a double bind.

C-28 Do you need any money to support your parents?

P-20 Not entirely. But you see I am going in the hole, financially. If I hadn't made this rash, completely idiotic automobile purchase two weeks ago . . .

P-20 P is "bragging" about his difficulties again.

C-29 How did that happen?

P-21 I went out to look at automobiles, not expecting to buy one at all. Then I saw one which I took a very irrational desire for. And I acted against every sensible impulse. It wouldn't be so bad if I were sure my present job would continue. And I want to go on with therapy; although I sometimes say I am on the edge of giving up, I don't really want to.

C-30 Do you think he makes progress in therapy? Do you feel he gets something out of it?

T-14 I think so, yes. As a matter of fact, up until the fiasco with the finals, P also felt he was making progress. Didn't you?

P-22 When I met Emily I felt fine. I felt confidence in myself. I felt that everything was going well for the first time with any woman. After the examination, I've been on the down grade ever since.

C-31 It seems still clear to me that he is working on an explosion, to avoid taking a stand and taking on responsibility. I don't think, however, that you would kill yourself.

P-23 No, I don't think I would.

80

T-15 But he entertained thoughts of committing himself. I pointed out that he could go to a sanitarium, have somebody take care of him, perhaps he could become a schizophrenic and prove that he was a complete failure. He brought that up in group psychotherapy that he was thinking about it, and one of the other patients said that it would be just like P to go and let himself be committed and then screw that up too.

C-32 (laughs) Wonderful.

P-24 Actually, buying this automobile was just as irrational as any psychotic.

C-33 Oh, that is the reason why you bought it.

P-25 I don't know.

C-34 You see, you want to hasten the moment of the explosion, you want to come to the end of your rope and then "get it over with," as people say. Then you may start anew again.

T-16 You are looking for a catastrophe.

C-35 Yes, a blow-up. And then it starts all over again. You see, life goes on just as well, and you will have to take a stand somewhere and sometime.

P-26 I think you struck the answer to something I wanted to know. I realize now no matter how contradictory my actions may be there is a consistency which I can see.

C-36 You are quite right.

P-27 So here was something which was diametrically opposed to anything that my own common sense would tell me was wise.

C-37 Right.

P-28 I could not figure out by myself for what purpose I did all that.

C-38 No, I know you couldn't.

P-29 Now I see the purpose. I want to explode. I want to ruin everything.

T-15 Here the therapist integrates a number of previous discussions and experiences with the main theme. The patient has also been concurrently in group therapy and psychodrama.

P-24 More "bragging."

P-26 This hammering at the main point under discussion is paying off; it is almost mandatory, once the correctness of the interpretation is established. It helps the patient to understand. He is by no means gullible, willing to accept anything he is told. On the contrary, he expresses his opposition very freely if he disagrees.

81

C-39 As quickly as possible, in order not to prolong the agony.

P-30 Yes, maybe you are right. I want to bring disaster on myself as fast as I can. That, I can see. But what purpose would that serve for me? That's what I don't see.

P-30 The patient is now groping for a better understanding once he began to see what he was doing.

C-40 You see, then all questions of passing your exams, of not having the ability for a job, of not getting along with a woman, all would be eliminated. Then you don't have to look for a job, don't have to bother with examinations, don't have to behave. A new life may begin, maybe as you said, as a drugstore clerk, or as an elevator operator, or something like that. "Let's wait and see where the explosion throws me. I will run away from home too, and then I am free with a new slate, like the man who is bankrupt and opens a new business."

P-31 In other words, then, I want to have an all inclusive alibi to cover all my failures.

C-41 Right.

P-32 That makes me feel better.

C-42 How come?

P-33 Now I know what I am doing, I didn't ... I surely didn't see that before.

C-43 (in reassuring tone) Well, we can't see ourselves.

P-34 But it still seems stupid to me. I know now what I am doing, but that is stupid.

P-32 This is an important reaction to an "understanding." The patient was puzzled before; the insight he gained gives some relief. But only momentarily. He immediately relapses into the pattern of self-accusation.

C-44 But why is it stupid?

C-44 This is an important therapeutic mechanism not to let the patient degrade and accuse himself, but rather help him to see

T-17 I think it's very clever.

C-45 It *is* very clever. I don't see anything stupid in it.

P-35 But who wants to fail? I don't really, I mean, consciously.

C-46 Now let us be realistic. You are sure that you cannot succeed. If you would pretend that you are capable, it would be much harder on your prestige if you then failed. But if you anticipate that you are no good and will fail, it is far less hard on your pride. In a certain sense you can be proud of your smartness that you knew in advance that it would happen, namely, your complete failure.

P-36 You know what fits in with that. Sometimes I have the urge of giving everything I have to my parents and get lost.

T-18 It seems to express your hostility against life. Things aren't going well . . . well, we just break everything up.

C-47 Yes, we have seen such situations.

T-19 People, like P, may reach the point where the only thing to do is to break up everything.

C-48 As if they would say, let's forget about it, have it over with. Then all the things we did in the past don't bother us anymore. Of course, they forget that life goes on. And the new situation may pose the same problem.

T-20 Yes, but if you declare bankruptcy, you get rid of all your pressures. You escape and . . .

C-49 Let the creditors fight among themselves.

the "logic" behind his apparent "irrational" behavior.

T-17 The therapist senses the importance of this turn of events; he adds his support, offsetting the patient's efforts to hide himself behind an assumed stupidity.

C-46 The "failure" behavior is explained as adaptive. This is another way of pointing out to the patient that you consider him intelligent, if misguided.

T-21 Yes, you know that is really a good way of handling tough situations.

P-37 Well, that's a way of figuring it out. Actually, this . . . could take about $100, move away from home and start all over again. That would accomplish what I want to do.

C-50 Have you ever had the idea that you would do it?

P-38 That's just one of the things I think about, but I don't actually do, like killing myself, or like trying to be an opera singer, all those things that . . .

C-51 But *that* you could do; it is within your reach. You probably won't do it, and that is the point. You may go as far as you think is safely possible, and at the last moment you will catch yourself. You may come to an explosion, but then you probably will get cold feet. You will settle down on a job, go on living as you did before, get in the same mess again, and have the same problems. That is not difficult to guess, because you will remain the same P and live in the same way.

P-34 I know.

T-22 Well, when you tell him he will be in the same mess, that may please him. I don't know what else P heard of what you said, but I am sure that he believed you that he will go on in the same mess.

T-22 The therapist senses the patient's reaction to what has been said. As the patient watches intensively while the two therapists talk to each other, so the therapist watches equally attentively what the consultant discusses with the patient.

C-52 You are probably right. But, keep in mind that it may interfere with his hope for an explosion. Until now he probably had this daydream of a possi-

C-52 Some may regard these statements as "moralizing." Actually, they have

84

ble explosion where he won't be in the same mess any more. And here he may be able to see that he can't escape the mess unless he takes some more constructive steps. The explosion never comes, and when it comes it still remains the same mess.

P-40 I know that.

C-53 You may play with the idea that you could escape the demands of life, but you can't. For this reason, some people wanted war. They thought they could leave all their problems, their wives and their jobs, their communities and their failures, and get into the army.

P-41 And yet, I do not want to be called to active duty.

C-54 Did you consider the possibility to volunteer?

P-42 Well, if I were desperate enough I might.

C-55 You see, war is the only form of a real explosion to get rid of problems which one cannot solve.

P-43 Maybe, to apply for active duty would serve my purpose, too. You see, being in the reserve I will get called sooner or later anyway.

C-56 There you have your chance for an escape.

P-44 Yes, I could apply for active duty. But I shudder at the thought of it. If I had to go, I think I would almost do away with myself. The army or suicide would be a very difficult decision to make, if I had to make them.

C-57 Why don't you want to join the army?

P-45 I can't — I mean I was in it enough — I mean, getting in the reserve was another one of those ways of ruining myself.

C-58 How come?

significance and importance for the patient; namely, that the explosion does not solve anything. He, like many others, believes that it does. For this reason, a more lengthy discussion and explanation of this point seemed necessary.

C-57 The lengthy discussion about the army does not concern the feelings of the patient about it, although these are revealed.

85

P-46 When I got out of the army, I didn't sign up for the reserve. I didn't want anymore of it. Then I got to thinking that I had better hold on to my Commission. If I did get back – I mean, if I had to go back because of another war, I would rather go in with a Commission – so I got back in the reserves. Now I regret having done it. If I had to get in again, I would get a Commission again, whether I was in the reserve or not, so I wouldn't have to get into the reserve for that purpose. The only purpose it will have will be this explosion that you are talking about. I can almost predict it. I will get some kind of a job, whatever I can get, and worry along until the army calls me, then everything will blow up.

The main point is the use which he makes of thinking about being recalled. This question is not directed toward getting information about his feelings or reasons, but about the role which this problem has for him in his present situation.

C-59 And then everything will be under control – everything is under control.

P-47 That's about what will happen.

C-60 See, you had everything figured out, even though you didn't know about it.

P-48 Not till you pointed out the pattern. Now I can see the pattern operating. The thing is this: I have been struggling, trying to break that pattern. I have tried it in all kinds of therapy.

C-61 There was a Viennese playright, a comedian. In one scene he makes fun of a hero who stands there and says, "now I will see who is stronger, me or me."

P-49 Yes, that's right.

C-62 You see that you were trying the same. You, too, are saying, "who is stronger, me or me. I'll fight against what I want to do and will see who is stronger, me or me . . . "

C-62 This is an example of what some call "inner conflict."

P-50 Well, so far the thing is that, intellectually, rationally, I don't want to be like that.

C-63 Well, is it so important that you think intellectually?

P-51 I wouldn't be — I wouldn't continue therapy, I wouldn't be doing any of these things if I were satisfied to be that way.

C-64 I can't agree with you. You know how long you have been in therapy and with how many therapists. Therapy fits in your scheme. It permits you to remain as you are and to pretend to have good intentions which you don't have. Everything is under control. It can go on for years and years. You always come close to an explosion, and somehow manage to go on. You are coming here and say that you want to be different. You have your therapy so that you can afford to remain as you are.

P-52 That's exactly what I sometimes think that . . . you seek, I've tried not having therapy, too. There have been periods of time when I wasn't going to anyone for therapy.

C-65 Did he interrupt for a while?

T-23 Well, for as much as three weeks or a month at a time.

P-53 Yes, I mean — I speak of therapy as what's been going on for the last five years.

C-66 Oh, I see.

T-24 Of which Adlerian therapy is his most recent attempt.

C-67 I see. How does it compare with your previous experiences, or do you have any impression as yet?

P-54 I would say I got more out of it, particularly in conjunction with psychodrama. Psychodrama is the most effective type that I've found, yet. And yet, as you say, "I'm still in therapy, so what can you expect . . . "

C-63 This statement characterizes our understanding of motivation. It emphasizes the importance of concepts and goals rather than of overt thoughts and feelings, which are only significant as movements toward a goal.

C-68 I don't know whether I would fully agree with you. I would rather say that you are not accepting the responsibility for your therapy.

P-55 That's what I mean by not getting well.

C-68 This interpretation gives a positive meaning to the patient's obvious tendency of accusing himself and of accepting readily "accusations" of others as valid.

C-69 You are well enough. I do not consider you a sick person. You are merely not willing to do what is necessary. But you are prefectly well.

P-56 Well, not being willing to do the things that are necessary to me is a very serious emotional illness.

C-69 This is a strong statement. Scientifically and theoretically it may require more careful consideration. However, it is made to counteract the patient's intentions to hide himself behind a feeling of being sick.

C-70 That's wonderful, now you have a label, you don't have to do the things that are necessary because you are sick anyhow.

P-57 But that's what I say, I use it as an excuse (C: of course you do), for not functioning.

C-70 The joking tone is still a part of the atmosphere of this particular interview. It is for the purpose of emphasis but it is not generally practiced.

C-71 Now we see what P thinks of himself. He has reached a new low. He is nothing, he had no chance to be anything. On the contrary, he almost brags about his inadequacy, and he has everything so prepared that whatever comes now is not his responsibility. "Let's wait and see what life will do to me." Well protected by the assumption of being sick, by being neurotic, he indulges in good intentions. But at the same time he wants to prevent doing harm to himself, and upsetting his life. He wants to get well by coming here. He constantly flaunts his good intentions.

P-58 The implication that I get from what you say is that I will never be any different, and there is no use trying.

88

C-72 Huh. Oh, no. Only in this way. If this form of trying, of demonstrating intentions which you don't have, continues, then there is no chance. Patients have stopped therapy because we didn't get anywhere, and long afterwards wrote, the ideas which we had discussed, began to take on form, and that they resolved their problems. All depends on when you will catch on. Right now you don't want to wake up. You want to continue messing things up. But you do not want to face what you are doing. You are here to function. You are not here to be concerned with your prestige, with doing what you like. You have to do what everyone has to do. To buckle down. This means to get a job, to act in accordance with the need of the circumstances, to participate in whatever life presents, and to — function. Of course, you have big ideas of what you want to be, what you could do. And you pretend that you will try. I have not the slightest doubt that in all your therapies and particularly here with T and psychodrama, you have already built up a tremendous fund, a foundation of proper perspectives which you could utilize at the right moment, and probably will use at the right moment. And then you will let loose of this whole super structure that you are no good, that you are sick and a failure, and that you have to mess up everything.

P-59 M-hm.

C-73 Now I would like to hear from you, T. What do you think about these things which we discussed? How does it fit in your discussions with P?

T-25 It fits in very well. I sometimes feel that what I am telling him is a little bit

C-72 A certain amount of moralizing is justifiable at this point; after all, therapy is directed toward the formation of new values. This lengthy discourse is the consultant's reaction to the preceding expressions of the patient's discouragement and defeatism. The elements of encouragement should be noted here: the example of other patients who finally caught on, the assumption of a beginning new orientation, and the possibility that he, too, can catch on.

T-25 Describes what the interchange has been

89

lost, because P always turns it into a self-accusation.

C-74 You are so right. P is a very tough customer, because under the disguise of recognizing his responsibility, he defeats you. He puts you exactly in the direction of what he wants you to say. Namely, what he should do, while he does nothing.

T-26 Yes, you are right.

C-75 Remember, we discussed it sometime ago, how difficult it is not to fall for his provocations. I am very sure that if I would work with him alone, it would happen to me too. I, too, might become impressed with him as being sick, no good and a failure. The crucial question is: Will he eventually convince us that he can do things well?

C-75 It is one of the advantages of interspersed double-interviews to keep the problems in focus. In a sequence of individual sessions, the therapist may yield to the insidious pressure of the patient. In the double-interview the therapeutic impasse becomes obvious and can be overcome. Such contest of convictions is found in most cases of therapy.

T-27 I am able to point out in the group last night how P inveigled Sally to give him hell when they all went out together after the previous group meeting. Then she was afraid that she may have hurt his feelings, whereas P, of course, ate it all up. It was a wonderful demonstration how P wants people to think that he is no good.

C-76 How easy it would be to put a label on that and call him masochistic or self-punitive. Actually, it is his glory when people get mad at him, look down on him, or help him. He keeps them all busy with him. He is in his glory when he can say, "Look how bad I am!"

T-28 And he acts accordingly.

C-77 You see, you have a different kind of badness. There are children who are bad; they are the toughguys. But they are brave and capable. That is not the kind of badness which P wants. He doesn't think he is enough man to be a tough guy. He is bad as a weakling.

C-77 Here the consultant turns suddenly to the patient. What motivated him was probably the introduction of the term "bad." It required amplifica-

between P and himself. By turning the interpretation into an accusation, P effectively neutralizes it.

90

"Look how weak I am, poor little me, I can't do it." Don't you think it's remarkable how successfully he can play weak?

T-29 And demand that others take care of him.

C-78 But that isn't all. You see, the only child, keeping his parents and everybody busy with him, and having always a special position, he is capable to continue that type of living. He keeps people concerned with him, feeling sorry for him, trying to help him, handsome as he is. So that gets him where he wants to be in life, different from the others. Other social workers get their examinations over and get jobs. He doesn't want to be like the others. First, he gets a job which is beyond his training, then he gets himself fired, and after all his successful studies he flunks in the last moment. You must admit that whatever you do, P, it is exceptional. You will find very few with a similar record like yours. You are very unusual, an unusual character, unusually weak, unusually incapable, while at the same time giving ample evidence of your capability, so that your failure becomes even more impressive.

tion. The discussion between the two therapists usually takes place only if some material has already been clarified to the patient, and is now worked over, so to speak. Consequently, the explanation of "badness" is directed toward the patient, so that he could not misunderstand it, and recapitulation of his feeling weak is again discussed between the therapists.

C-78 Here reference is made to the life style. This basic information is repeatedly applied to situations as they come up to help the patient understand why he is what he is. It generally entails a summation, a short review of the total situation. Again, as long as well understood material is reviewed, the consultant addresses himself to the therapist. As soon as a new idea comes up, which, at this point, is the idea of being exceptional, he addresses himelf again to the patient.

P-60 I guess the thing for me to do is make up my mind that I am that.

C-79 On the contrary, that you are *not* that. You already have made up your mind that you are *that,* namely, an unusual failure. You do not have to make up your mind about it, you have already decided to be that.

P-61 And you think that I should just go ahead and not unconsciously, but consciously try to do that?

C-80 Now that would be progress, if you at least dropped the policy of pretense. That would be some kind of progress.

P-62 And yet, consciously I can't (C: But of course) bring myself to do what I apparently want unconsciously.

C-81 You are right, because you do not want to take on the responsibility for what you plan and what you want.

C-80 This is a crucial point and therapeutically extremely significant. In dropping the pretenses of not wanting to do what he is doing, the patient would be forced to take on responsibility which he shunned through his pretense. It is obvious how the patient tries to extricate himself from this realization.

T-30 If you would admit that you only *play* a weakling, you would no longer be one.

T-30 In this crucial moment the therapist steps in and makes an excellent clarification of the point under discussion, also directing himself to the patient. It is such interplay which makes a double-interview so much more effective than a single interview.

C-82 And because you pretend to be a weakling . . . in order to play the role of the weakling, you have to pretend that you *want* to be strong, you ought to be

C-82 At this point the teleological approach, characteristic of Adlerian Psychology,

92

strong. The whole purpose of being a weakling and all the benefits you derive from it, are lost if you admit to yourself that you *want* to be a weakling and for what reasons. What kind of a weakling could you be if you would openly admit that you want to be weak because it pays? You can only play weak if you say, "I want to be strong, and look how weak I am!"

T-31 You know that explains the seeming discrepancy in P's character. Something you can't understand if you look at his life's history. How he has achieved certain successes and then had horrible failures. This whole picture becomes immediately clear as soon as you realize that P is trying to demonstrate his weakness and to gain a special place through it.

C-84 He is quite impressive by always coming close to getting somewhere, and then he has to mess it up in order to seem weak.

T-32 As if he is saying, "Look how hard I try, and can't. You can't accuse me of not trying."

P-64 I cannot allow myself to succeed in anything. I have noticed that.

C-85 Of course, we know it.

P-65 I come to the edge of success and I do something to fail.

C-86 Exactly. But do you know why? If you would succeed, you would be like anyone else, because, after all, you would not be a spectacular success. But in your sudden failure you are spectacular. And you could not maintain your assumption of weakness if you really succeeded. Then you merely would be a man like anyone else.

T-33 He comes close to it. He comes close by almost getting his Masters.

is emphasized; an attempt is made to impress the patient with his obvious "private logic."

T-31 Again, the therapist moves in when a trend of thought comes to an end. He introduces a new point for discussion, at the same time following up the material covered so far.

P-64 The intensely listening patient contributes some conscious observation to support the interpretation of his private logic.

C-87 But he cannot even succeed in failing because when everything seems lost he suddenly gets a spurt and pulls himself out of the predicament.

P-66 The thing is that I am miserable in the process.

C-88 Are you surprised about that? How can you expect to be happy if you fight against life, if you don't want to be like others? Of course, you are bound to be miserable if you operate according to your plan. Everyone who would try to have his own way by being weak and be different in this way from everyone else, would be miserable.

P-66 Again, the patient who accepts and understands the explanation goes one step further; he understands why he is doing things, but cannot see why he should suffer if he does what he wants. The ensuing discussion deals with an important aspect of our interpretation of neurosis.

P-67 T has often pointed out that I take pleasure even in my misery and I can see now that my misery serves a good purpose for me.

C-89 It again is something special, it makes you something special. The others around don't suffer as much.

P-67 It is obvious that the patient's beginning insight is the result of many previous discussions of the same point. He is not quite sure, yet. Here he remembers that he had almost recognized the purpose of his misery, while in his preceding statement (P-66) he was rather perplexed by it. This process of seeing and forgetting is part of a process of learning.

T-34 Yes, why should you give it up, P?

C-90 It seems that you can be sure that whenever you will try to be a success you will come close to success, and whenever you try to be a complete failure, you will come close to failure.

P-68 H-hm.

T-34 This is a very frequent form of emphasizing dramatically the patient's private logic, and challenging his motivation. The therapist again stepped in in a crucial mo-

C-91 You never will make either of them. That seems to be your style. You will not fit in either group, into those who succeed, not those who fail.

T-35 You will be even a failure in being a failure.

C-92 Isn't it a pity? He can't even succeed in being a failure. I think today we really took him apart.

T-36 I think this was a productive interview.

ment and in an impressive manner.

T-36 This statement is made without asking the patient's reaction to the interview. The term "productive" needs an explanation. Obviously, it does not imply that the patient was unusually productive in bringing up new material. What makes this interview productive is the clarification of certain fundamental issues and dynamic processes which are pinpointed. They are thereby presented as a basis for future single interviews which will elaborate the various points. But more than that: this double-interview climaxed a series of rather dull and stagnant single interviews. Both the therapist and the patient received new impetus for more intensive work.

Chapter 10

Three Excerpts from Double Interviews

These three excerpts from double interviews show various aspects of the process: A double interview to assess progress in therapy, another in which the therapist asks for help from the consultant in dealing with a particular problem and a third in which the consultant falls into a trap and is helped out by the therapist.

In each of these excerpts, one can see that where either consultant or therapist is insensitive, the other is able to be sensitive and keep the therapeutic process going.

A double interview can be used to assess the patient's progress in therapy. The following patient had complained of feeling worse after the previous double. The excerpt shows the reason for this and resolves the problem. In this session, the patient reported a dream in which she experiences many difficulties but persists and succeeds in solving a problem. The consultant responds to the dream by interpreting it as a sign of improvement. The segment begins with the consultant responding to the dream and searching for a relationship between the dream and the patient's current life situation.

Both therapists are male and function as equals in the double. The patient is female. In this segment, the consultant is insensitive at first and the therapist and patient both work together to clue the consultant in.

C-1 T, P is feeling better. Is she considering breaking out in any way? . . . changing her life in any way?	**C-1** C is responding to a dream reported by the patient. He addresses T.
T-1 Uh . . . starting a new job . . . starting a new enterprise . . . uh, she's a little afraid of that . . . afraid that it's going to snowball . . . afraid that it's going to get out of hand . . . and she won't be able to handle it. It's going to become too successful.	**T-1** Reports the patient's fear.
C-2 That last should be the worst fear she has, it seems to me . . . She was also feeling better last time I saw her with you. Since that time has she continued to make strides?	**C-2** Has not been sensitive to T's hint. He persists in focusing on the demonstrated improvements.
T-2 Uh, yes, uh . . . I'd like to follow her reaction to that because she had a particular kind of reaction after our last talk when we felt and we told her that she seemed to be doing things better and getting well . . . No? What was it?	**T-2** Draws C back to the parent's distress . . . T responds to P's interruption.
P-1 I felt lousy after the last double session. I thought of it because you told me I was getting better. You both seemed to agree I was getting better. But I haven't made up my mind, yet.	
T-3 Mm, hm.	
C-3 Think you're feeling lousy after the session meant wait, I'm not getting better yet.	**C-3** Now C finally tunes in and pays attention to the distress.
P-4 I just don't feel what I felt four years ago. I feel better than I did seven months ago.	
C-4 Mm, hm!	
T-4 One of the things she said was she was afraid that we were going to dismiss her . . . because we said that she was getting better. . . . seemed to be doing better. She was afraid that we were going to throw her out.	**T-4** T now elaborates.
C-5 Yeh, which may be another way of saying she's not completely well, yet . . .	

	that she wants to be completely well.		
P-3	I do? or I don't?	P-3	P is not certain how to
C-6	You do! ... I said that you do.		view her own feelings.
P-4	I do.		Her therapists seem
T-5	Suppose we assure you that we are not		to have a higher opi-

T-5 Suppose we assure you that we are not going to kick you out . . . You do have problems although we also feel that you are making some strides.

P-3 P is not certain how to view her own feelings. Her therapists seem to have a higher opinion of her progress than she has herself.

P-5 All right! I feel I am, too. There's no question about it. I don't feel, though, that the big test has yet come. When I initially came into this office there was a fear of doctors. In other words, I had nothing to go to a doctor for, but if I had to, would I be the spastic idiot that I've always been? That's what I want changed! ... I know, you don't believe me.

P-5 One of her presenting symptoms had been severe anxiety whenever she had to go to a physician's office – for any reason at all.

It is characteristic of P that she does not expect the therapist to take her seriously.

T-6 No, I really am trying to understand what you say, because from time to time, you come in and you say, uh, "gee, it doesn't bother me . . . I'm not worried about cancer or things like that."

P-6 But that's not true, I still am.

T-7 It's not true?

P-7 No!

C-7 You still have the same fears?

P-8 Yes, I'd like to be able to go into a doctor's office and not be afraid. What I'm saying is that this is a very significant point to me.

C-8 I think you're right. That would be the test.

P-9 For me! I don't know if it's the right test. That's the way I rationalize it . . . I don't know if it's even right or wrong. Maybe it's a smoke screen or something but it's very important. Even to feel well, you have to go to a doctor. The idea that maybe he's going to find something wrong. And not be frightened by that . . . Now that's . . .

T-8 The point where you know that you're well.

P-10 Yeh, is that wrong?

T-9 No, I don't see it as a question of right or wrong. It's the test you set for yourself

C-9 I don't think you're off . . . I don't think it's wrong to want to not have neurotic fears.

P-11 Yes! All right fine. That's what I said . . . I'll come in here and talk about anything you want to talk about. That, to me, happens to be a very significant thing, though.

C-10 Granted.

P-12 I would like it to some day not be so significant in my life. Everybody walks in with apprehension . . . there's no question about it . . . I know this to be true, but not the way I walk in to the doctor.

T-10 The thing that you feel to be significant is not the thing that we feel is significant.

P-13 No, I told you I agree with you and I see where it is a side-show . . . I still say, though, that's a very real thing to me.

T-11 It's important.

P-14 It's important. It's my criteria . . . not a complete . . . completely being well but it's a very important part of being well.

C-11 If I can conquer this, even 50% not a hundred per cent – even 10% . . .

T-12 There's a difference right there because she is lowering the percentage. She used to keep it up to 80-90%.

P-15 Or a hundred . . . you're right . . . because you said something to me once that doing something . . . that something . . . I can't remember exact-

T-9 T accepts P's standard for herself. This is done because it shows respect for the patient's own point of view and is intended to show support.

T-10 T here refers to previous interpretations about the meaning of the symptom.

P-13 Interpreting the symptom as a sideshow is a common Adlerian interpretation. The acute phobia is often a displacement – a "sideshow" created to divert attention from some other issue. At the same time, the sideshow also reveals in metaphorical terms what the issue actually is.

100

ly . . . you'll feel 10% better. It's the truth. I'm less afraid than I was, but by the same token I'm still afraid. I cannot say that by tomorrow I'll go to my physician and walk in there and not shake, that's all.

T-13 Uh, do you like this physician?

P-16 Yes, of course!

T-14 What do you think about him personally?

P-17 I know him personally.

T-15 Aside from his skill . . .

P-18 Yeh, he's a very nice guy. He thinks I'm crazy!

T-16 The reason I bring this up, C, is because of the particular way that she sees us . . . you and I. Uh, if I reveal to her any, uh . . .

P-19 Imperfection.

T-17 Imperfections, or point out any which may be your imperfection or your humanness . . . something that I have in common with everybody else . . . she doesn't want to hear about it. She said . . . she's even admitted it . . . she doesn't want to hear us talk about anything that indicates that we have something wrong with us. I wonder whether she feels the same way about . . .

P-20 My doctor? No! No! Very strange. Mm, Mm.

T-18 So he's not only skillful but he's a human being.

P-21 What does that make you? (Laughter). It's the truth, though.

T-19 C, I wonder how this fits in with the way she was brought up? . . . being a model kid! . . . Always to be strong and do the right thing, 'n everything else. She also expected it of other people. Apparently, it sounds like she's expecting it of us, also!

T-16 Certain patients do not wish their therapists to be less than perfect. Such patients often have some form of anxiety as a prominent symptom. P seems to be searching for some kind of perfect security.

T-19 T refers to material previously determined about P.

C-12 Well, she was brought up with the idea that people have imperfections, but wants to fight that as much as possible.

P-22 There's a difference between fighting them and covering up. Isn't it right to fight?

C-13 Sure it is . . . sometimes even right to cover up. But sometimes it isn't necessary to cover up . . . sometimes it isn't necessary to fight because imperfection is simply a human quality. . . . . It doesn't have to destroy!

P-23 It goes back many years. The more perfect you try to become the more you're unsure about what imperfections are normal. How do you know the difference?

> P-23 P puts into words one of her core problems. Since one cannot tell the difference, one can never be sure one is normal.

C-14 I believe it's a matter of judgment.

P-24 How do you acquire the judgment?

C-15 Most people learn it.

> C-15 This is an encouraging statement. If most people learn it, perhaps P can also.

P-25 And what if you can't learn?

> P-25 Refuses to be encouraged at this point.

C-16 Why do you think you can't?

P-26 Well, I haven't.

C-17 Or if you can't make the judgment you can ask other people.

P-27 But the people you ask are the people who supposedly know.

C-18 Maybe that's why you want us to . . .

> C-18 C now has an insight of himself.

P-28 Be perfect!

C-19 To be all wise when it comes to human behavior.

P-29 Isn't that right?

C-20 I can understand it . . . it makes it easier for you to trust our judgment if we seem to be perfect.

P-30 I'm not asking you to make decisions for me . . . but I'm obviously using this therapy as a . . . somewhat as a guideline or am trying to . . .

C-21 That's appropriate.

P-31 If you're not right, where am I? You know, maybe I'm being flip about it but . . . I mean . . . is it wrong for me to set you up like this? . . . if I'm here for help?

T-20 Would it help you if you do that?

P-32 Would it help?

T-21 Yes, would it help you?

P-33 Well, of course it would help! How could it not?

T-22 I guess patients see us in all different kinds of ways. You say this is the way it would help you if you saw us as not having any defects and knowing all?

P-34 Aw, look I know you do . . . when you talk about physical things that I equate them with . . . just the total situation . . . I don't think I make myself very clear!

C-22 I don't think we have trouble understanding you nor are we objecting, particularly to what you're doing . . . it really isn't an issue between us.

P-35 As long as I do it with you . . what if I do it with other people, then it becomes more of an issue.

C-23 Well, look . . . if I went to a lawyer I would want to believe that he knows everything there is to know the law.

P-36 Especially, if it were a serious case.

C-24 So T and I don't object to it . . . we understand!

P-31 In line with her lifestyle, P still wants to make sure she is doing the right thing.

T-20 Meaning to want the therapist to always be right.

P-35 Again P wants to be sure she is doing nothing wrong.

C-24 Reassures P again.

The following protocol is an excerpt from a double interview in which a female therapist brings her female patient to a double session with a senior male consultant. The patient is involved in a relationship with a married man and the therapist feels this relationship is essentially destructive for the patient. The consultant, without disagreeing with the therapist's opinion, clarifies some of the patient's motives in maintaining the relationship.

C – Consultant (Male)
T – Active Therapist (Female)
P – Patient (Female)

C-1   Well, P . . . T . . . It's been a while since I've seen the two of you together and you've been seeking each other regularly . . . What's been going on in Therapy?

C-1   A common way to start and a common concern for the C. Note that he addresses his opening question to both of them. This patient has previously been a hospital in-patient after an acute depression with a suicide attempt by overdose.

P-1   Well, (chuckle) I'm going to get the giggles.

P-1   The patient has not seen the consultant recently and is embarrassed. This will pass.

T-1   First of all, the kind of things we anticipated didn't seem to happen. P, correct me if I'm wrong, but we were concerned perhaps P wouldn't make it with a female. I haven't experienced any trouble at all relating to P, and she seems free with me.

T-1   A previous concern had been that P would have difficulty relating to a female therapist.

P-2   Right . . . much more so than I think I was with a man. I don't know whether it's that there is no barriers where you get yourself tied up with a man or involved with a man or something. There's just no barriers . . . I guess it's kind of like, uh . . . well, I'm getting

104

closer to women anyway ... more female friends ... so I suppose that has something to do with it, too.

C-2 More female friends ...

P-2 Uh Hm ...

P-2 Another concern was that P had very limited relationships with female peers.

C-3 I'm not really sure, P, but one of the things I remember from your life style was that your competitor was a male, in one sense, and a female in another sense.

P-3 Right!

C-3 C makes a connection between the past and the present. The life style hopefully reveals styles of behavior and styles of relationships (characteristic patterns)

T-2 Who was the female?

T-2 It occasionally happens that C recalls a detail better than T.

C-4 Mother.

P-4 My mother.

C-5 Well, I guess T is just a good therapist, anyway.

P-5 (Chuckle, chuckle)

T-3 I'm glad that's on tape.

P-6 (Chuckle, giggle) ... give you two points!

T-4 As a matter of fact, I've enjoyed her company and I've enjoyed being with her.

P-7 Yeh, right!

C-6 Do you think it would mean something to P that she was being enjoyed, not exploited? ... Just enjoyed?

P-8 Yeh, it did ... as a fact, the funny thing is that I said to someone the other day, I said, "You know, the strangest thing happened ... I think the thing that meant more to me than anything else was when we were sitting here last time and T said something about my assets, and you said, "I think, you know, that she's open and honest and that's why

T-3 & T-4 It is appropriate in Adlerian therapy for the therapist to express common appropriate feelings when their expression shows the therapist's "humanity" in a positive way. This is not considered excessive countertransference.

C-6 C interprets although he is actually addressing T.

P-8 This certainly seems to indicate that the patient feels accepted by T.

105

I like her." kind of gave me a nice secure feeling. You know, rather feeling that you're coming in, you know, you're paying out money or they could really care less, one way or the other . . . you're just, you know . . . there.

T-5 We have been talking about P's relationship with J, the married man, you know. For a while she didn't see him, but they're seeing each other again.

C-7 Well, how do you feel about that?

C-7 Addressed to T.

P-9 I know what I think of that . . . I don't approve of that at all. Not at all . . . because there actually is no gratification, whatsoever. It's just pure aggravation to myself . . .

C-8 You're telling me that it's all aggravation.

P-10 Oh, sure, I think it would be in the end.

C-9 Is there any satisfaction, at all?

C-9 C assumes that if P continues the relationship, it must have *some* meaning to her. His questions demonstrate a dialectical method used by Adlerians. Their intent is to help the patient explore her own motives.

P-11 Yeh, there is.

C-10 What satisfaction?

P-12 The satisfaction of still being with someone that I enjoy and talking with someone that I enjoy.

C-11 Well, if you enjoy him, what's the aggravation?

C-11 C already knows the answer but he is "setting up" the statement of the problem — the conflict that results from the combination of enjoyment and aggravation.

P-13 Because I will never, I doubt seriously, that in the near future at any time that I'll be able to be alone with him or end up with him or that, you know, that he'll change in any way. I don't think he will.

C-12 Could you put in one sentence what is it that you want and you're not going to get?

P-14 I would like him and I will never get him. I know that, you know. But just sort of hang on and keep my hopes up, you know, I'll go on seeing him and maybe having breakfast with him, talking to him on the phone . . .

C-13 What does he really mean to you?

C-13 Asking for continued clarification.

P-15 Uh . . . I have many different opinions because emotionally, it's a person that I love very much. You know, intellectually he is a very screwed up individual. It would not be good for me.

C-14 Is there any possibility that the fact he is a screwed up individual makes him more attactive to you.

C-14 C suggests an interpretation with which both P and T disagree.

P-16 Do you think so, I don't think so.

T-6 No, I agree with her, I don't think so.

P-17 No, because to me he's a very strong person, I told T this week . . . we kind of balance each other out. When he has problems we sit down and talk about it; when I have problems we sit down and talk about them and help each other out . . . we did help each other out . . . we had fun together, just being with each other . . . just enjoying things. You know, and I don't think . . . the problem is we both really still can't handle it. He can't and I can't because even on the phone he says, "Well, I know I should never talk to you again . . . never call me again and I'll never call you again" and I says, "Hey, you're making promises you're not gonna keep," and he says, "I know, but I enjoy talking to you." He feels the same way I do. He still enjoys, you know, talking to me, and everything, and I do, too.

P-17 P points out what she considers positive in the relationship.

C-15 I see him intending to maintain the relationship. And I see P intending to maintain the relationship. Now, I think, possibly both of you can get hurt

C-15 C now moves to a related issue in preparation for the interpretation he will

107

in the encounter but P is our patient and we have an obligation to her in terms of the potential destructiveness of the relationship, I agree with you, T. I see no good coming out of this thing. The only good thing that came out of it was that P learned that she could be in love.

T-7 It wasn't the first time . . .

P-18 It was the first time that I had ever been this strongly in love.

C-16 Or maybe it's the first time she ever felt strongly enough about a man to want to be his woman. She may never have had that kind of relationship before, with anybody.

P-19 I made a few immature mistakes, you know, but I think I found out that I could be satisfied with one person.

C-17 That is an important thing to find out.

P-20 Yeh.

T-8 I see P right now as a girl who is ready to get married.

C-18 My life has progressed now where I'm up to the point where I did have a relationship which I think is the most serious that I have had and, yeh, I would say that probably the next person that came along . . . if the timing and the situation were right, I don't think I would hesitate getting married like I did before.

C-19 I see . . . what the two of you are saying is, you have stopped being afraid of marriage itself, as marriage.

P-22 I think I still have the old fears but I am not afraid that somebody is not going to help me along with it or that I am not going to be able to conquer it with somebody else, you know.

C-20 You mean you can be a woman, hum?

P-23 Well, yeh, the only reason of being afraid of marriage is that of being

make in C-16. Note that C is focusing, as he has been, on the process of therapy as it is going on in the transactions between T and P.

C-16 To speak to T about P in the third person is a multiple therapy technique. P hears herself talked *about*. It is a device for sharpening P's attention in preparation for the series of interpretations to come.

T-8 This is not a change of subject. P's image of herself as a person and as a previous topic of discussion between T and P. Here T understands C's direction of movement and comes in on the same wave length.

P-23 This is probably an important insight for

108

afraid of failure . . . and I am really not afraid of failure now. I'm much more secure than I was. I still don't think my husband will be totally faithful 'n everything . . . I don't think there's any man who really is . . .

C-21 You don't think there's any man who really is?

P-24 It really isn't that much of an issue, you know, as long as he doesn't want a steady girl friend. I'm not afraid of it anymore.

C-22 What T is saying, then, is T feels that would be the time for you to start meeting other men.

P-25 Right! We have gone over meeting other people and where to meet other people and I have friends fixing me up and I am going out and I just don't . . .

C-23 Sounds like it's hard work.

P-26 It is . . . it really is! I don't . . .

T-9 Wait a second . . . Wait, you want to talk about how she stays in this potentially destructive relationship. Maybe she is too busy to find other men.

C-24 Well, I think that this is a very important issue, that P sees herself ready to make trouble for herself, knows with full consciousness that she's doing it, and is still doing it, and is wondering why she's doing it when she knows what she's doing.

P-27 Yeh, I mean I've broken up other relationships, you know, and you know, really cried, and everything under the sun and gotten stoned outta my head and the whole shot and I've never

the patient.

T-9 Here the active participation by T keeps the interview from getting off the track. This is an example of how each therapist watches the interaction between the patient and the other therapist.

C-24 This is the key behavioral issue that requires explanation.

109

picked up the phone to call the person
. . . oh, I cried for about a week or so
and then I'd go about my merry
business and I ended up being very
good friends with these individuals and
never really wanted to go back or if we
did go back, fine, it was no big thing.
This is a different situation. This is a
situation where I'm really like holding
out my hand and saying, "Go ahead,
slap me, in my own eyes . . . and he is
doing the same thing to . . . we both
are.

T-10 Do you want to have the power to hurt
him?

P-28 Not hurt him physically or anything
else but the power to confuse him and
upset him, yes, tremendously.
Remember when I told you that when
I walked into his office that night he
looked at me and he said, the only way
out was to kill me and kill himself . . .
That's pretty sick and pretty desperate.
He maintains now that he can talk to
me and he knows the closeness isn't
there. I know it is, otherwise he
wouldn't keep calling. When he calls, he
calls three or four times a day.

P-28 This also shows what
is probably an impor-
tant insight. The
desire to reach
another person by ag-
gressive behavior is a
compensation for feel-
ing powerless to reach
him strongly enough
in affectionate ways.

T-11 P, have you got the strength to tell him
not to call you anymore? . . . that you
don't want to see him, anymore?

T-11 T is opposed to the
relationship since it
will only lead to prob-
lems for P.

P-29 No!

T-12 What do you think you're going to do?

P-30 I think I'm probably going to see him
and it will probably upset me a little
bit, but I'll slowly work my way around
that this is the way it is, and that he
"Loves his wife" and that he is going to
stay there and that that's going to be
it for the rest of his life and as a happy
individual. I'll just have to learn to accept him as a friend or, you know, just
get to the point where if he calls, fine,

P-30 P seems to agee with
T's reasoning but
affirms her intention
to continue the rela-
tionship with T.

and if he doesn't call, fine . . . you know, one way or the other.

T-13 How are you going to do that?

P-31 Uh, I don't know . . . it just comes with time eventually. It's a realization. The realization is there but time, I guess, will kind of take care of it.

T-14 Then you won't have to do anything but just wait.

P-32 Well, I won't pick up a phone and call . . .

T-15 I mean, for your feelings to change.

P-33 I'll be going out and I'll be doing things. I'm not going to sit home and be moody about it and sit and stew about it.

T-16 How long do you think it will take?

P-34 I don't know.

T-17 Mm . . . you know . . . a year from now?

P-35 Yeh, that's a good approximation.

T-18 Six months?

P-36 Yeh, about a year . . . closer to a year . . . six months to a year.

T-19 Closer to a year?

P-37 Yeh . . . maybe sooner . . . I think it . . .

T-20 I sure wouldn't want to look forward to one year of suffering.

P-38 I think it depends on another thing, too . . . I think it depends on how fast someone else comes along.

T-21 Who has to come along? . . . you or him?

P-39 No, no, no, . . . I think it depends upon how fast someone else comes along who is an outside person, where I'm concerned.

P-31 "I guess time will take care of it" usually means, "*I'm* not going to make any changes at this time."

T-16 This is a common technique used by Adlerians. P is asked to estimate how long it takes her to make a decision that she herself admits she must eventually make. The therapeutic purpose is to show P that she herself delays taking a positive step and instead chooses to continue suffering. Sometimes, one may use exaggeration to make the point; as in, "Do you think it may take you ten years." The patient's answer is usually a protest that he does not intend to wait that long.

Sometimes the technique also has the effect of helping the patient to see himself as actually making

T-22 If you got yourself all emotionally involved with this man, how can an outside person come along?

P-40 I'm still opening myself up to outside people.

C-25 We have to start bringing this to a close and what the two of you are doing, as I see it, is getting side-tracked down a track that won't have any satisfactory conclusion because P *does* expect to keep looking around for other people while she maintains the relationship with J.

P-41 Right!

C-26 Since P seems to be accepting the fact that it will not work in the long run with J . . . "I may get some pleasure out of it, but I will also get pain . . . therefore, I have to prepare myself for looking elsewhere . . . " T, you seem to be thinking . . . Oh, my God, why doesn't she stay away from this guy . . . he is poison to her . . . why should she go back into it a little longer? If she keeps him around the less available will she be for other men. I would like to have her break this relationship entirely. Now, what T says has logic behind it, of course, and it shows the concern for your welfare. What you are saying, P, is understandable and I think, fits in with the kind of person you are, and I think it gives us an opportunity to make a therapeutic interpretation to help P see something else about the

plans for his behavior in the future ("choosing") at the moment when he consciously feels helpless in the grip of the situation or of his feelings.

T-22 Another example of T's disapproval of the relationship.

C-25 "What the two of you are doing . . . " C thus assigns responsibility to both T and P. The purpose of this is to confirm that the process of psythotherapy is a mutual collaboration between therapist and patient.

C-26 As C talks he addresses first one and then another. He is now leading up to the main therapeutic interpretation of this interview. C is concerned that the therapy will suffer because T's aim of persuading P to end the relationship with J runs counter to P's desire to continue it. In such a situation, the potential for therapeutic impasse becomes large. T is likely to continue to suggest an end to the relationship. P will

112

kind of person she is, and it's a kind of sad thing. I bring it up, now for purpose of making anybody feel sad but because I think it's important to recognize something, here . . . That, deep down, when you try to discover how P feels, one of the things that you find is that she feels deprived, and unloved.

P-42 Sure.

agree with T's reasoning but her underlying intention to maintain the relationship will be enforced by what Adler called a counter-compulsion; i.e., she will experience strong emotions that will negate the effects of T's reasoning and keep her involved with J. Thus, P and T will have opposing goals, a situation that encourages therapeutic resistance.

C-27 And the person that loves her and said that he would consider killing her and himself is a very, very valuable person in her life because her parents never cared that much about her . . . and nobody else did either. These are the things that get through to P even though she may say, "I know it's poison, but it's all I've got. This guy loves me" . . . and she can feel a strong bond toward you because you accepted her and she doesn't expect this kind of thing in life and when it happens, she's not willing to let it go, because it was what she always wanted and her parents always held out to her but never gave her . . . or very rarely!

C-27 In order to heighten the effect interpretation of the behavior, C first reviews P's feelings in a reflective way. The purpose is help P feel understood.

P-43 Yeh, it makes sense, yeh!

C-28 So, it's not going to be easy for P to give up the feeling that somebody really cares about her and give up this caring person, until either somebody else cares about her, which is what P thinks or, what is more important from my point of view as a therapist, until she cares so much about herself that she

C-28 This is an example of an Adlerian interpretation. Feelings of deprivation, of being cheated, of being unloved are, to the Adlerian, subjective conclusions and are all

113

stops feeling deprived . . . Because the feeling of deprivation stays with you no matter now many people love you. As soon as they leave the room, you feel deprived.

P-44 Right!

C-29 It's the feeling of . . . "but I don't need someone to love me all the time to give me a sense of worth" that means you don't ever have to feel deprived again.

P-45 That explains . . . like . . . the whole thing!

forms of the "inferiority feeling." While the original childhood origin of the feeling may have been within reason, the later adult feeling has little to do with reason. Horney has discussed this well in her discussion of "neurotic claims" which are irrational and insatiable.

Note that C tried to interpret that the feeling of deprivaton is irrational . . . "stays with you no matter how many people love you. As soon as they leave the room, you feel deprived."

C-29 The person who depends on someone else's love in order to feel worthwhile, can never feel secure unless he has constant repeated assurances that he is loved and unless he feels *in control* of the person upon whom he depends. In Adlerian language to be dependent means to want to control the other through "weakness." See again K. Horney who talks about the "neurotic claim" for love and about "morbid dependency."

114

C-30 All right, I think this is a good point at which to stop. I feel that good progress is being made by the two of you.

T-23 You made me feel kind of sad.

C-31 About what?

T-24 You made me understand how P feels.

C-32 And why you are so important to her?

T-25 Yes, and I can understand how it is difficult for her to give up that kind of relationship.

P-46 I can, too, which I didn't understand before, but now I also see why it's hard. Maybe that'll help to make it a little bit easier.

C-33 Maybe. O.K.

T-26 Thank you, C.

P-47 Thank you (sigh)

C-30 A good time to stop a session is when a definite moment of insight appears. It would be a mistake to introduce a new topic at this point and also a mistake to belabor this one.

The following segment shows how a consultant can fall into the trap of overintellectualizing with the patient and how the therapist may sometimes have to rescue him. All the participants are male. The patient has had several years of therapy with another therapist and feels he did not gain anything except to feel less obligation to please his mother. He professes to be unhappy with his life, but makes no plans to change it. He does not like his business, but he is expanding it. All efforts to lead him in any direction have only increased his indecision. This double interview was scheduled especially to try to change the directon of therapy – to help him to decide whether he would change, would accept the status quo, or would continue to do what he was doing and complain about it at the same time.

Therapist and consultant function as equals in this interview.

P-1 I enjoy it because it uses most of my abilities . . . you know . . . it requires that it test my mettle . . . it requires a rather wide range of my talents . . .

T-1 Aside from testing your ability it is something to enjoy. Also it doesn't take much energy to do . . . You actually do enjoy it.

P-1 The patient is discussing his current occupation.

115

P-2   I enjoy it . . . I enjoy the income I have from it. There are many things about it which I don't enjoy but there are many more that I do enjoy. Sometimes I regret that it isn't doing much for the world . . . and it doesn't put me in contact with very exciting people; yet there are things about it that I enjoy . . . but I'm sure that it would be the nature of many things that I did, so it is not the business that is unpleasant . . . it's the fact I would like to do that which is outside of my life that would make life more pleasant for me.

P-2   This segment shows how the patient constantly weighs pros and cons of his situation, thus creating an ambivalence which keeps him from being content with himself or from making any changes. The end result of all his ruminations is maintenance of the status quo.

C-1   You're not blaming the business, then?

T-2   No.

C-2   And you even enjoy the business? . . . to a certain extent.

P-3   Right. I don't think I came here indicating that everything I was aiming at was changing my business. In fact, I think really, the opposite. I think, yeh, if I were able to make myself more of a . . . If I were able to be less committed to less secure things . . . I can see myself doing other things than business.

P-3   The ambivalence continues. Any statement by C or T which tends to reduce the ambivalence is countered by more expression of indecision by P.

T-3   What would you do then?

P-4   Teach school . . . find a job which didn't require that I . . . you know, . . . that gave me some challenge . . . that didn't face me with uncertainty.

C-3   And you have to work because you like money and the things that it will buy for you.

C-3   C tries to pin P down.

P-5   I mean, that I haven't really accomplished the next trick which is to come to find that to be the most important thing.

P-5   P successfully avoids the pin.

C-4   So, you've got all these materialistic tastes and you're working hard . . . you have to work hard so that you can just retire on your income?

C-4   Another attempt to pin P down.

116

P-6 No, that's not true . . . I really don't. I had a birthday Friday and I'm faced with the realization that there's little material goods that I still want to get.

C-5 You don't want much more than that?

P-7 In effect what occurs . . . that's intriguing . . . yeh, I'd almost have to say is that what I do like most is that it keeps me busy.

C-6 You're caught on a road that you didn't choose . . . it's just a road that you can keep walking on?

P-8 Yeh! My temptation is constantly that when you say things like that is to say that "isn't everyone."

C-7 Shall I respond to the fact that you said it or that you attempted to say it? Or shall I respond to the fact by saying that it is typical of you to do something and not do it at the same time? That's the pattern we're talking about.

P-9 Yeh.

T-4 He used to say he likes a direction . . . that was all very important to him, and he liked to have some kind of guidance. He's saying that he's sort of got a direction that he just backed into or he got into the pattern without knowing he was choosing it.

P-10 So have I created a double-sided situation? . . . under which I do both, as you say?

C-8 That's what I think . . .

P-11 The dilemma . . .

C-9 Well, you see it is as a dilemma and I don't deny it as a dilemma. I see something else there, as well . . . that is . . .

P-12 It is a dilemma!

C-10 Yeh! You can do both or none! . . . as you please . . . and you maintain your own freedom and you don't commit yourself or pin down to anything or

P-6 Avoiding the pin.

C-5 Another attempt.

P-7 P again avoids by shifting his ground.

C-6 C tries again.

P-8 P reveals his opposition.

C-9 C tries to counter P's attempt to remain bogged down in indecision and discontent.

C-10 C tries to point to the purpose of the "dilemma." In Adlerian theory, such a dilem-

117

anybody . . . because even while you're busy doing something you can always claim it is not really what you want to do! And, as long as you claim *that,* you are claiming an exemption . . . Now, I think that I want to make one thing clear, that this is not a conflict you're having with *us* when I try to get you to commit yourself to *anything.*

P-13 No, No! I think what I said was that I would have to respond to you . . . I'm responding to myself . . . that's a repetition of the same . . . of the pattern that I'm aware of . . . I mean, when I question that myself, my response is the same.

T-5 He certainly has had the opportunity . . . life has put him in the position . . . where he could have responded or changed directions at any moment but he essentially refused to . . . and he and I have talked about a specific set of tasks . . . choosing a place where he should live, getting involved in the community, marriage, etc.

C-11 You brought those things up or has P brought them up?

T-6 I brought them up.

C-12 And what has P done to you?

T-7 P said that has been beaten to death already and said yeh, I know that . . . (Laughter) Oh, I knew that already.

P-14 Sometimes, it's therapy . . . o.k. toss me another one . . . let's see how I can beat the next one to death (Laughter)

ma is an indication that the patient does not have intention to resolve the situation, but to claim special exemption because of a "dilemma."

C-11 C and T can talk to each other in front of P and perhaps P will understand what he is doing. When they have been speaking to P directly, P has automatically defended himself.

P-14 P seems to capitulate.

C-13 Well, that's what both of you started talking about the beginning of the interview . . . what you seemed to be saying P was "I am having a lot of therapy and therapy is very good, interesting and very successful." . . . You, perhaps have the feeling that your life should change in some way but if we think about the ways your life may change, what do we think about? . . . Well, obviously we think . . . if he doesn't like the work why doesn't he get another job . . . or if he wants more money why doesn't he work harder . . . or if he wants a permanent relationship why doesn't he get married . . . or if he doesn't want to get married why doesn't he let himself swing and stop worrying about it? . . . So we say, "Well, why don't you?" and you can play the "Yes, but" game in answer. I suppose we've finished playing that game and we don't recognize the old question of change as straw man . . . it is maybe not even necessary . . . not even required . . . maybe not even important or desired. The notion of change is a monster that you seem to be struggling with but you're really struggling with trying to decide what to do with P or if you want to do anything with P or just wait . . . wait it out . . . maybe it will go away. If you wait long enough maybe you won't have to do anything and for you to have to do something is like an onerous burden . . . it is very unpleasant for you.

P-15 Why do I feel I should be committed to something?

C-14 You call these things commitment . . . what I see is you don't have the freedom to act . . . you are inhibited and don't dare do something. I still see the

C-14 This interpretation is from material previously revealed by the lifestyle.

119

little boy that's afraid to take a chance for the consequences. You have glorified that into "why make trouble?" . . . 'I'll keep things running smoothly . . . I'm on top of it right now." We require nothing of you. We do not require change. I feel that you have hemmed yourself in and, therefore, you feel you should change and, therefore, have to justify not changing.

P-16 That undoubtedly is true! . . . and is really the essence of my situation. That doesn't . . . uh . . . I did it . . . (Laughter) Uh . . . (silence) . . . then, I can't think . . .

P-16 Insight! P catches himself trying to obfuscate matters again. After he catches himself, he finds himself at a loss for words.

T-8 You don't have to yes, but . . . don't argue it . . . just do something!

P-17 O.K. but I'm not arguing it.

T-9 My point is logical and is most likely correct.

T-9 T takes advantage of the fact that P is a logic-chopper.

P-18 Yes, it is!

T-10 It may even be 100% correct? Then why argue against it? (Laughter)

P-19 O.K. tho I accept your logic. It is not related to changes that can be involved . . . that can be the real question . . . about myself . . . that I had allowed myself to become terribly inhibited. I had no idea where to proceed from there.

P-19 His usual ruminations set aside, P now is at a loss what to do.

T-11 Why proceed anywhere?

P-20 Well, I want to change it . . . because it's obviously discomforting.

C-15 In what way is it discomfort?

C-15 C is trying to pin P down again.

P-21 Unless I really get pleasure from the guilt I'm experiencing, . . . the pattern of not doing.

T-12 How does it make you uncomfortable?

P-22 Because of the guilt . . . unless I really do get my pleasure from the not acting, therefore experiencing guilt, then I'm experiencing guilt or discomfort because I'm not acting.

P-22 P begins to intellectualize again.

120

C-16 How does it sound to you that he gets his kicks out of his guilt?

C-16 Addresses T.

T-13 That's one of the possibilities we must consider.

T-14 Do you care if he gets married?

C-17 No.

T-15 Do you care what neighborhood he lives in?

C-18 Doesn't matter to me.

T-16 Why don't we give him permission not to change?

C-19 We'll take the guilt on ourselves!

C-19 This is not an attempt to relieve the patient of guilt. C and T both treat the guilt as another straw monster that P has created and not as the real problem.

P-23 It can't be the only one side of the discomfort because I'm 36 years old and doing nothing.

C-20 What if we say you don't have to change! We accept you the way you are!

P-24 But I don't accept me the way I am! (chuckle)

T-17 Then what would happen if you were to accept yourself the way you are?

P-25 I would use all these other options of defending myself by not being the way I am . . . I'd use the option of . . . uh . . . complaining about the situation I'm in . . . consequently experiencing the displeasure of not doing anything.

P-25 This, of course, would not be actual self acceptance. C and T are not succeeding in shaking P's position.

C-21 Al right, we have to start coming to the end of the session and as usual at a time like this, we have to look ahead and see . . . where we are going . . . what are we doing . . . what are we trying to achieve? . . . Well, there's never been any question P about your intellectual ability to handle the concepts and neither has there been a question about the effort which you put in, in therapy; I think it's important for all of us to recognize that one of the goals you have in therapy to delay action rather than act. Therapy helps you *not* to do

C-21 An attempt to structure the next session.

certain things. Therapy is a justification for not doing certain things.

P-16 It's the additional phase of the uncomfortable . . . fact that I am aware that I shouldn't be struggling.

C-22 We can not in any way choose your goals for you, nor do we have to, but we also do not necessarily agree with what you have chosen as your goals; that is . . . that you *have* to change . . . to make a decision about the business, get married, all those other things! As long as we are your therapists keep our stand in this regard, then maybe we won't fall into the trap of trying to get you to change.

P-26 Protests that he is still suffering.

C-22 These were the patient's stated goals on entering therapy.

T-17 We're not going to get him to change. We accept you as you are, realizing at this time you can not accept yourself . . . and you don't know what to do with that . . .

P-27 Begin with the premise of you accepting me as I am and that I should accept myself as I am . . . Now you see, I'm playing the game again . . . so my responses are always to see how far I can get you to go . . .

P-27 Insight! P catches himself again isolating affect from thought by trying to start a purely intellectual discussion.

C-23 You will try to get us to suggest the next step . . . so that you can defeat it.

C-23 Interpreting the power contest between P and the therapists.

P-28 Right!

T-18 P, you're basically a guy who does things for other people. Maybe you feel that you don't deserve to be happy.

P-29 I feel more strongly than I did in the past that I deserve to be happy.

P-28 P admits at this point that he uses therapy as a chess game between himself and the therapist. His problem still exists but it now seems obvious that the way he has been trying to solve it will not work.

C-24 Well, you work hard. You're seldom frivolous and when you're frivolous, you feel guilty about it.

P-30 All right, haven't you just made a judgment, though? That's a heavily weighted statement of my situation.

C-25 No!

P-31 You say you accept me as I am.

C-26 Yeh!

P-32 That was heavily weighted on the side which is on the side of me which says I'm obviously tied in knots and unable to respond to the joys and pleasures of life and . . .

T-19 Heh, that was a very interesting interaction because he was careful to, uh . . .

C-27 He tried to trap me?

T-20 He tried to trap you, heh! He staked it out.

C-28 I think I got out.

T-21 No you didn't.

C-29 Well, I can't win them all.

T-22 O.K. Then the process of therapy is to be on this subject for a while.

P-33 My impression is that we should be more goal oriented.

C-30 We will do our best to satisfy you . . . tell us (Pause)

T-24 Yet, do you notice . . . very carefully . . . how very carefully P avoids to set up a structure?

P-34 Hmmm . . .

C-31 I really think that this is what therapy is to you . . . sort of muddling through on a foggy night. Is that discomforting?

P-35 Yes, it is. I've got a little saying from a newspaper saying "some people are never happy unless they are miserable."

C-24 This has been established in previous interviews.

P-30 P sets the trap. C is unaware.

C-25 C falls for the bait and enters into the philosophical, logic-chopping agreement.

P-32 P springs the trap. He is back to the interminable discussion which leads to no action.

C-27 C doesn't see it yet.

T-20 T points out the trap.

C-29 C succumbs.

P-33 A suspicious sounding statement from a patient who has been avoiding action.

T-24 Since P does not answer, T interprets his silence.

P-34 Hopefully there is some insight.

Appendix

INDICATIONS AND CONTRAINDICATIONS

Sometimes neither patient nor therapist is willing to accept an innovation in therapy and multiple psychotherapy occasionally meets such resistance. Rarely, two therapists simply cannot work with each other and it would be harmful for the patient to have them as a therapy team. A patient may be congenial with one therapist of a pair yet may detest the second therapist. Life is full of such contingencies but they do not seem to outnumber the usually difficulties of establishing a therapeutic relationship. So it has been our experience that the difficulties of practicing therapy with a team approach are no greater than practicing alone and that the benefits of the team more than outweigh any of the drawbacks.

This conclusion is supported by some independent decisions made by three therapists who were trained in psychotherapy by the authors and who are now well established in their own right. They are Carol Lefevre, Ph.D., Leo Lobl, M.S.W., and Dorothy Peven, A.C.S.W. We mention their names because the two lists that complete this small chapter are their doing. Together, the three for their own sakes, constructed the lists of indications and contraindications for the use of multiple psychotherapy. They have listed sixteen indications and twelve contraindications. The lists are in their own words, exactly as they handed them to one of the authors. As teachers we are proud when our students learn well and we are indeed proud of these three. By this time they are no doubt better practitioners of multiple psychotherapy than their teachers.

We have made no changes in these lists because none were required. They are an eloquent enough statement made by three "junior" therapists – a third generation of multiple therapists. Their expressions are terse, sometimes fortuitously slangly and to the point. Their language will be understood by anyone who has ever been a therapist.

LIST 1
INDICATIONS FOR MULTIPLE THERAPY
FOR BOTH THERAPIST AND PATIENT

1. For training (inexperienced) therapist.
2. Inexperienced therapists may feel more comfortable.
3. To secure another opinion about a particular approach being used or when another opinion would be useful in interpreting a particular piece of behavior.
4. When the therapist needs to extricate himself.
5. In a busy practice it is simpler to meet emergent situation when there is an unexpected absence.
6. Confirmation for patient and therapist that therapy is on the right track.
7. When consultation needed, when other therapist more conversant with particular aspect of therapeutic intervention.
8. When the patient reaches an impasse in therapy and something must be done to break up the impasse.
9. When the patient needs confirmation about a particular interpretation.
10. If the patient is not satisfied with the way things are going in therapy.
11. When it is therapeutically important to make every effort to shorten therapy, multiple therapy can be impactful and dramatic and possesses possibility of being very freeing for the patient.
12. When dealing with a passive patient, participation in multiple therapy is hard to resist. It's most intriguing for the patient.
13. When it is appropriate for the therapists to role play in front of patient a particular life problem relevant to the patient.
14. When it is especially important for patient to feel accepted — supporting social network.
15. When it is important to demonstrate to patient that two people with differing opinions can work out resolutions of differences. Patient can see cooperation on his behalf.
16. In dealing with a clinging vine, it is easier to discourage "transference." Prevents overdependence on one therapist. Not to be interpreted as putting patient off as we want and must involve the patient in the solution to his problems.

LIST 2
INDICATIONS AGAINST THE USE OF MULTIPLE THERAPY
1. When the therapist himself is not clear or not sold on the value of this approach.
2. If the therapist feels insecure in his activity with the patient, exposure may be too threatening.
3. When two therapists are in competition and there is a manipulative patient on the scene.
4. If one therapist is determined to be an observer and not an active participant in the multiple therapy process.
5. When there is marked difference in goals or marked difference in methodology.
6. If one of the therapists decides to go on an ego trip.
7. If the patient decides that the therapists are ganging up on him.
8. When there is no clear view as to the purpose of multiple therapy in the minds of the therapist(s) as well as in the mind of the patient.
9. Extremely willful patients who for one reason or another are determined to manipulate and may want to change therapists – their hobby is to defeat therapists.
10. When a child may feel adults are ganging up on him.
11. If therapists do not have mutual respect for one another.
12. If patient is dead set against it.

Appendix II
THE LIFE STYLE INVENTORY
Harold H. Mosak, Ph.D.
Bernard H. Shulman, M.D.

Name _____

Date _____198__

On this page list siblings in order of age and ask for a spontaneous of each sib as a child. Give age differences between sibs.

1	2
3	4
5	6

SIBLING RATINGS

Most different from respondent: How?
Most like respondent: How
Groupings (age, sex, etc.)
Which played together?   Which fought each other?
Sickness, surgery or accident?   Unusual talents or achievements?
Respondent's childhood fears?   Respondent's childhood ambitions?

	Most to Least		Most to Least
Trait Inventory		Cheerful	
Intelligence		Sociable	
Grades		Sense of humor	
Industrious		Considerate	
Standards of achievement		Bossy	
Athletic		Demanded way	
Daring		Got way	
Looks		Temper	
Feminine		Fighter	
Masculine		Chip on shoulder	
Obedient		Sulked	
Made Mischief		Stubborn	
Openly rebellious		Shy	
Covertly rebellious		Sensitive and easily hurt	
Punished		Idealistic	
Standards of right-wrong		Materialistic	
Critical of others		Methodical – Neat	
Critical of self		Responsible	
Easy going		Withdrawn	
Charm		Excitement seeker	
Pleasing			
Add other traits as responses suggest			

PHYSICAL DEVELOPMENT

Include any features not coverd by previous questions.

SCHOOL INFORMATION

Include most liked and least liked subject; best and worst subject.

SOCIAL INFORMATION

Peer relations and role in peer group during childhood and adolescence.

SEXUAL INFORMATION

Include menarche, puberty, early experiences, sexual preferences, feelings about own gender role.

PARENTAL INFORMATION

FATHER Age Occupation	Favorite? Why?
Spontaneous description	Ambitions for children?
	Relationship to children?
	Sibling most like father? In what ways?
MOTHER Age Occupation	Favorite? Why?
Spontaneous description	Ambitions for children?
	Relationship to children?
	Sibling most like mother? In what ways?

NATURE OF PARENTS' RELATIONSHIP

OTHER FAMILY INFORMATION

Include family's role in community, family values, atmosphere, stability of family. Ask for mental illness in family.

ADDITIONAL PARENTAL FIGURES
Grandparents, other adults

EARLY RECOLLECTIONS

1. Age

2. Age

3. Age

SUMMARY OF FAMILY CONSTELLATION

SUMMARY OF EARLY RECOLLECTIONS

ASSETS

Bibliography

Baruth, L. and D. Eckstein. *Life style: What it is and how to do it.* Dubuque, Iowa, Kendall – Hunt, 1978.

Dinkmeyer, D. C., W. L. Pew and D. C. Dinkmeyer, Jr. *Adlerian counseling and psychotherapy.* Monterey, Calif.: Brooks/Cole, 1979.

Dreikurs, R. Psychological differentiation of psychopathological disorders. *Individual psychology bulletin,* 1944-5, *4,* 35-48.

Dreikurs, R. Techniques and dynamics of multiple psychotherapy. *Psychiatric quarterly,* 1950, 24, 788-799.

Dreikurs, R. The psychological interview in medicine. *American journal of Individual Psychology,* 1954, *10,* 99-122.

Dreikurs, R., H. H. Mosak and B. H. Shulman. Patient-therapist relationship in multiple psychotherapy II: Its advantages for the patient. *Psychiatric quarterly,* 1952, *26,* 590-596.

Dreikurs, R., B. H. Shulman and H. H. Mosak. Patient-therapist relationship in multiple psychotherapy I: Its advantages to the therapist. *Psychiatric quarterly,* 1952, *26,* 219-227.

Dyrud, J. E. and M. J. Rioch. Multiple therapy in the treatment program of a mental hospital. *Psychiatry, 16,* 21-26.

Fiedler, F. The concept of the ideal therapeutic relationship. *Journal of counsulting psychology,* 1950, *14,* 239-245.

Flescher, J. *Dual therapy: Triadic principles of genetic psychoanalysis.* New York: D. T. R. B. Editions, 1966.

Ganz, M. *The psychology of Alfred Adler and the development of a child.* London: Routledge and Kegan Paul, 1953.

Getty, C. and A. M. Shannon. Co-therapy as an egalitarian relationship. *American journal of nursing,* 1969, 69, 767-771.

Greenbank, R. K. Psychotherapy using two therapists. *American journal of psychotherapy,* 1964, 18, 448-499.

Hadden, S. B. The utilization of a therapy group in teaching psychotherapy. *American journal of psychiatry.* 1947, *103,* 644-648.

Haigh, G. and B. L. Kell. Multiple therapy as a method for training and research in psychotherapy. *Journal of abnormal and social psychology,* 1950, *45,* 659-666.

Haley, J. *Problem-solving therapy.* San Francisco: Jossey-Bass, 1973.

Hayward, M. L., J. J. Peters and J. E. Taylor. Some values of the use of multiple therapists in the treatment of the psychoses. *Psychiatric Quarterly,* 1952, *26,* 244-249.

Herschelman, P. and D. Freundlich. Group therapy with multiple therapists in a large group. *American journal of psychiatry,* 1970, *127,* 99-103.

Hill, L. B. and F. G. Worden. Participant teaching of psychotherapy by senior physicians: A hospital program and clinical findings. *Psychiatric quarterly, 1952, 26.*

Hulse, W. C., W. V. Lulow, B. K. Rindsberg and N. B. Epstein. Transference reactions in a group of female patients to male and female co-leaders. *International journal of group psychotherapy,* 1956, *6,* 430-435.

Lazarsfeld, P. F., B. Berelson and H. Gandet. *The people's choice.* New York: Duell, Sloan and Pearce, 1944.

Lazarsfeld, S. Dare to be less than perfect. *International journal of Individual Psychology.* 1936, *2,* 76-82.

Lazarsfeld, S. The courage of imperfection. Journal of Individual Psychology, 1966, *22,* 163-165.

LeFevre, C. Training therapists. Panel on multiple therapy. Paper presented at annual meeting North American Society of Adlerian psychology. Chicago, May 26, 1977.

Lehrman, N. S. The joint interview: An aid to psychotherapy and family stability. *American journal of psychotherapy,* 1963, *17,* 88-93.

Levinson, B. M. *Pet-oriented child psychotherapy.* Springfield, Ill.: Chas. C. Thomas, 1969.

Lott, G. M. The training of non-medical cooperative psychotherapists by multiple psychotherapy. *American journal of psychotherapy,* 1952, *1,* 440-448.

Lundin, W. H. and B. M. Arnov. Use of co-therapists in group psychotherapy. *Journal of consulting psychology,* 1952, *16,* 76-80.

MacLennan, B. W. Co-therapy. *International journal of group psychotherapy,* 1965, *15,* 154-166.

McKelvie, W. and U. Friedland. *Career goals counseling: An holistic approach.* Baltimore: FMS Associates, 1978.

Mintz, E. A. Transference in co-therapy groups. *Journal of consulting psychology,* 1963, *17,* 34.

Mintz, E. A. Male-female co-therapists. Some values and some problems. *American journal of psychotherapy.* 1965, *19,* 40-53.

Moreno, J. L., *Psychodrama,* New York: Beacon House, 1946.

Mosak, H. H. Evaluation in psychotherapy: A study of some current measures. Unpubl. Ph.D. dissertion, Univ. of Chicago, 1950.

Mosak, H. H. Early recollections as a projective technique. *Journal of projective techniques,* 1958, *22,* 302-311.

Mosak, H. H. Predicting the relationship to the psychotherapist from early recollections. *Journal of Individual Psychology,* 1965, *21,* 77-81.

Mosak, H. H. Life style assessment: a demonstration focused on the family constellation. *Journal of Individual Psychology,* 1972, *28,* 232-247.

Mosak, H. H., The controller: A social interpretation of the anal character. In H. H. Mosak (ed.) *Alfred Adler: His influence on pyschology today.* Park Ridge, N. Y.: Noyes Press, 1973, 43-52.

Mosak, H.H. and R. Gushurst. Some therapeutic uses of psychological testing. *American journal of psychotherapy*, 1972, (26), 539-546.

Mosak, H. H. and B. H. Shulman. *Life style inventory*. Chicago, Alfred Adler Institute, 1971.

Mosak, H. H. and B. H. Shulman. *Individual psychotherapy: A syllabus*. Chicago: Alfred Adler Institute, 1974.

Paulson, I., J. C. Burroughs and C. B. Gelb. Cotherapy: What is the crux of the relationship? *International journal of group psychotherapy*, 1976, *26*, 213-224.

Peven, D. E. Multiple psychotherapy: Adlerian method. In *International encyclopedia of psychiatry, psychology, psychoanalysis and neurology*. New York: Aesculapius Publishers, 1977, *7*, 382-384.

Reeve, G.H. A method of coordinated treatment. *American journal of orthopsychiatry*, 1939, *9*, 743-747.

Seidler, R. and L. Zilahi. The Vienna child guidance clinics. In A. Adler and associates, *Guiding the child*. London: George Allen and Unwin, 1930.

Shulman, B. H. The family constellation in personality diagnosis. *Journal of Individual Psychology*, 1962, *18*, 35-47.

Slavson, S. R. Discussion. *International journal of group psychotherapy*, 1960, *10*, 225.

Sonne, J. C. and G. Lincoln. The importance of a heterosexual co-therapy relationship in the construction of a family image. *Psychiatric research reports*. American Psychiatric Association, 1966 (20), 196-205.

Treppa, J. A. Multiple therapy: Its growth and importance. An historical survey. *American journal of psychotherapy*, 1971, *25*, 447-457.

Treppa, J. A. and K. G. Nunnelly. Interpersonal dynamics related to the utilization of multiple therapy. *American journal of psychotherapy*, 1974, *28*, 71-84.

Wainwright, W. H. Treatment of paranoid disorders by dual therapists. *Current psychiatric therapies*, 1966, *6*, 105-109.

Warkentin, J. Partners in psychotherapy. *Voices*, 1967, *3*, 7-12.

Warkentin, J., M. L. Johnson and C. A. Whitaker. A comparison of individual and multiple psychotherapy. *Psychiatry*, 1951, *14*, 415-418.

Watterson, D. J. and S. Collinson. Copsychotherapy of the individual patient. Indications and operative factors. *American journal of psychotherapy*, 1976, *30*, 608-622.

Weisfogel, J. and M. Sirota. Dual simoultaneous interviews: A research approach with the psychotic patient. *Psychiatry*, 1968, *19*, 313-323.

Whitaker, C., J. Warkentin and N. Johnson. A philosophical basis for brief psychotherapy. *Psychiatric quarterly*, 1949, 23, 439-443.

Whitaker, C., J. Warkentin and N. Johnson. The psychotherapeutic impasse. *American journal of orthopsychiatry*, 1950, *20*, 641-647.

Yalom, I. D. and J. H. Handlon. The use of multiple therapists in the teaching of psychiatric residents. *Journal of nervous and mental disease*, 1966, 141, 684-692.

Index

resistance discussed in, 21;
    planning the next steps, 23;
  multiple, variety of experiences for patient, 28
  structure, 13;
  summary, 23
introducing patient to multiple psychotherapy, 19-20
introspection, 16
"ironclad logic of social living," 10

Lazarfeld, S., 22
learning about oneself, 55-56
LeFevre, Carol, 53, 125
Lehrman, N. S., 4
life situation, 14
life style, 9, 11, 13, 15, 16, 19, 20, 41, 57;
  behavior in consonant with, 15;
  brought to psychotherapeutic session, 41;
  clarification of a patient's, 15
  exploring the, 15;
  formulation interview, 57;
  as group of convictions, 15;
  knowledge of one's own, 41;
  reference to, 16;
  set of statements explaining patient's behavior to him, 20;
    summary of main points, 19
Life Style Inventory, 128-134
life tasks, exploration of, 14
Lobl, Leo, 125
Lott, G. M., 3, 51
Lundin, W. H. and B. M. Arnov, 39, 48

marriage counseling, 5
McKelvie, W. and U. Friedland, 15, 57
method of teaching, 52
Mintz, E. A., 39
mirror technique, 16, 22
morbid dependency, 114
Mosak, Harold H., 15, 55, 57;
  and R. Gushurst, 43
motivation, 14, 15;
  for seeking treatment, 14;
  patient learns about, 15;
movement, 10, 16;
  confronting patient with his, 16;
  toward others, 10
multiple interviews, a variety of experiences for patient, 28

multiple psychotherapy,
  according to interpersonal dynamics, 4;
  advantage for patient, 31-35;
  advantage to therapist, 27-29;
  affect on emotional attachments, 35; feelings of "desertion,";

vis-a-vis other, 43-44; of each therapist to the other vis-a-vis
    patient, 48-49; to therapists as dyad, 37;
    reluctance of, 6;
    use the appropriate therapist for, 40
Paulson, I., 5
perceptions, consensually validated, 11; subjective, 11;
    of threat, 11
periodic recapitulation, 23
personality, as result of training, 10
personalities of two therapists, difference of, 21
Peven, Dorothy, 4, 125
playing devil's advocate, 28
post-session review, 47
post-therapy sessions, 4
prearranged signal, 47
prestige, 10, 17,
private goals, therapist's own, 41
private logic, 11, 13, 16, 22, 28;
    confronting patient with his, 16;
    therapist argues from point of view, 28;
    therapist presents the patient's, 22
proper therapeutic relationship, establishment and maintenance of, 11
psychological investigation, 9, 13;
    objectives, 13;
psychotherapists disagreeing, 4
psychotherapy, 11, 15;
    diagnostic and therapeutic aspects, 15;
    a learning process, 15;
    uncovering, interpretive form of, 11;
psychoses, 8
psychotic patient, 7
purpose, 9, 15, 23
    in a double interview, 23

reeducation, 9, 11
Reeve, G. H., 1, 7
relationship,
    between psychotherapists, 4;
    each therapist to other, 44-48;
    each therapist to other vis-a-vis patient, 48-49;
    each therapist to patient, 40-41;
    patient to one therapist vis-a-vis other, 43-44;
    patient to therapists as dyad, 41-43;
    transference, 37, 40
reorientation, 11, 16, 23,
resistance, 1, 12, 23, 26, 113;
    prevented or eliminated through discussion, 23
respect, 13
responsibility, 16, 34;
    increased awareness, 16;
    through participation in discussion, 34

144